# SENTNESS

## HOW APOSTLES HELP US TO BE APOSTOLIC

### Bob and Mary Bain

## Open Wells Publishing

Copyright © 2021 by Bob and Mary Bain
All rights reserved
ISBN 979-8-50878-020-3

Shilbottle, Northumberland, United Kingdom
Bob and Mary Bain
e-mail: bobbain@hotmail.co.uk

# SENTNESS

## HOW APOSTLES HELP US TO BE APOSTOLIC

# CONTENTS

# POEMS

## Prophetic Pictures

There are thirty-four pictures in this book which we have chosen carefully to say something. We think God will speak to you through them, in your own context. As you read the book, when you come to a picture, ask Him what He might be saying to you from the picture.

The full list of images with acknowledgements is on page 221 Colour versions of these pictures can be found in the Resources section of our website, **welcomenetwork.org**

# In appreciation of:-

All those who have brought their experience, wisdom and friendship into our lives, especially our family.

Amongst them, we would like to especially thank
Hugh Osgood, Robin Jegede-Brimson and Gary Seithel for their pioneering example and inspiration.

The Welcome Network Team:-
Alicia and Gabriel Osinibi, Christen Forster, Michael Osinibi, Freda Brobby, Vikki Harrison, Steve and Gemma Carder, Ann Franklin, Rachel Bangura, Talia Havana, James and Andrea Fraser, Gabby Llewelyn, Nigel and Susan Moore, Alex Shoderu, Amanda Thomas, Max and Vickee Bawhom and all our supporters.

Our friends in Churches in Communities International, the Inter Prophetic and Apostolic Alliance, and Ekklesia Arise.

In Northumberland, Tyne and Wear:-
Alan Dickinson, Andy Raine, Robert Ward, Paul Merton, and Peter and Theodora Adegbie.

Also our thanks to the
Prayer Net team:- Sandra Stuart, Joan Gladders, Fay Renwick, Jane Dawson, Phil and Frances Harding,
Open Wells Planning teams:- Lynne and Doug Gowland, Andrew and Michelle Duff
Creative Mission Team:- Aaron Shah and Paul Revill.
David Forster and all in the Pockets Conversations.

Last but not least – our friends in Alnwick and Shilbottle, especially those involved in the Awake Gospel Community Choir, Ana MacKay and everyone in Bright River Chapel, and friends of the Albafarne Prayer Garden.

# FOREWORDS

I have been involved in many expressions of Church life throughout my ministry and I can say two things with confidence: firstly that the Church needs to rejoice in its diversity and secondly that it needs to fulfil its mission with an ever-growing sense of hope.

I first saw hope and diversity come together in a powerful way in the late 1960s and early 1970s when some of the evangelistic enterprises I was engaged in, in my teens and twenties, became infused with hope through the Charismatic renewal. Not everyone appreciated the effectiveness of this combination of confident evangelistic zeal and a fresh emphasis on the Holy Spirit's empowerment, and there were times when each thought the other to be a distraction. But through it all hope rose high. Right now I sense a fresh rising of hope in the Church and we need to do all that we can to encourage it and build on it.

One of the things that made a real difference back in the 60s and 70s was the fresh appraisal of the Ephesians 4 ministry gifts. We have now had five decades to search the Scriptures and to improve our understanding. We have left aside our grandiose notions of lordly apostleship and our overly authoritative prophetic assertions, and through the wisdom of experience have learnt to move together in greater love, humility and harmony.

This book on apostleship by Bob and Mary Bain is the product of such wisdom. It is sensitive, inspiring and timely. I want it to bring fresh hope to the Church in exactly the way that Bob and Mary intend. I honestly don't think they could have expressed their case any better.

So now, as we, the Church, in all our diversity continue to learn from one another, we need to declare boldly that not only is there hope *for* the Church but there is about to be so much hope *in* the Church that we are surely on the brink of seeing it once again spill over to transform the world.

*Hugh Osgood*
*President, Churches in Communities International*

--------------------------------------------------------------------------------

The subject of the apostolic, and the gift of apostles to the church, is very much a word in season right now. God is restoring the fullness of the five fold ministry ascension gifts to His church. I believe the last one of these to be restored in our time is the gift of the apostle to the church; it's not enough for the church just to recognise someone who has an apostolic gift, the church needs to receive the person/gift. There is a great nervousness in the church, particularly in the UK, around the restoration of the apostolic that needs to be overcome. Correct alignment to apostles needs to take place; they are a gift from Jesus to His church. It is a very biblical pattern of how church should function correctly.

I am delighted that Bob and Mary have spent time putting this book together and I believe it brings a balanced insight into the gift of the apostle. I hope this book will reduce the fear around this amazing biblical gift. Jesus himself is our great apostle; He demonstrated **Sentness**.

*Very Reverend Alan Dickinson OSL*
*As One North East*

Paul is quite clear, in Ephesians 4, that there are those given by Jesus as apostles (verse 11), from his ascension (verses 8-10), as gifts to the church. And that these apostles will last until the church has reached full maturity, as measured against Christ himself (see verse 13). The problem is that we often confuse these Apostles of the Ascension, with the Apostles of Jesus' incarnation (The 12 and possibly 72 specifically "sent" during Jesus natural life), and the Apostles of the Resurrection (which included women and family members like James, Gal.1:19). In the two centuries following Pentecost, we find early church references to a host of apostles given from Jesus' ascension. They even warn how to spot false ones, (a warning that wouldn't be needed if all apostleship had stopped after the original batch died).

Apostles are a key ministry in the church. It is sadly just the abuses of perceived power and spiritual jealousies that have confused the issue. Apostleship is not glamorous; its proof is found in the health of the church communities, which have been served by apostles, in a host of different ways. (1 Cor.9:2).

Bob and Mary have been serving communities in this way for as long as I have known them; they don't try to collect them, or demand an allegiance of thanks from churches. Their commission has come from Jesus; it is his "well done, good and faithful servant!" that they are looking for. And so, Bob and Mary are well qualified to offer their thoughts on this foundational and pertinent ministry. At times of reformation, we need apostles to help us find new shapes for church and to join congregations together, in ways that express Jesus more fully than the sum of their parts.

As you read their observations, I would encourage you to look to the Lord for yourself, and borrow the words of a privileged young Israelite: "Here I am LORD, send me" (Isa.6:8). It's not about power or glory, but there is always an anointing that comes with His commission.

*Christen Forster*
*jesuscentred.org/e/resources/*
*supranatural-life.com*

-----------------------------------------------------------------------------------

Amazing!
I so love this in-depth, scholarly, yet beautifully down to earth, pragmatic work by Bob & Mary...
As I opened it up and looked at the title and subtitle, my *spiritual* mouth began to water. *"As the deer pants for the waters so my soul pants after thee.."* pens the Psalmist (Ps.42), and again, *"He prepares a table before me.."* (Ps.23)

Bob & Mary lay a crystal-clear foundation for their well-lived out, personal and amiable expression of ministry, with the subtitle, 'How Apostles Help Us to be Apostolic'; as they echo and trumpet the call to all standing apostles to fulfil the mandate - to *"equip the saints for the work of the ministry"* (Ephe.4:11). For those so graced with this pivotal New Testament ministry, the whole, massive, raison d'être of <u>being</u> an apostle is to ooze out the key characteristics of apostolic ministry, thereby infecting others!

Apostles are called to unapologetically ooze and transmit 'SENTNESS' to everyone around them, with the apostolic spirit carrying and reflecting the heart of DADDY GOD, releasing the SPIRIT of GRACE and walking as the LORD JESUS walked.

'SENTNESS' crucially imbibes the spirit of divine commissioning, from where the word apostle originates.

In this well laid out and skillfully built writing, we feel the warm mantle of the apostle embracing us and encouraging us to grow in Grace and Authority. We discern the metron (aka 'measure of rule and influence', see 2 Cor.10:13) in our own lives increasing, as we imbibe and hearken to the apostolic spirit. And with the help, urging and urgency of the HOLY SPIRIT we embrace the apostolic mandate to GO beyond our present borders, introducing change, advancing the Kingdom, and pursuing Calling; because we too are SENT.

As the precious words of this 'parchment' alight on people's minds, souls and spirits, I humbly discern ahead of time, the Precious Holy Spirit softening and renewing the wineskin of many hearts, preparing them for the next phase of their growth in Christ, with a Holy embracing of 'SENTNESS', to new levels and fresh pastures.
Amen and Amen – so be it!
Much love in CHRIST,

*Robin Jegede-Brimson*
*Inter Prophetic & Apostolic Alliance.*
*Author "The Blaze of Transition"*

# PREFACE

*'A green shoot will come up from the stump of Jesse; from his roots a Branch will bear fruit'* **(Isa.11:1).**

## THE CHURCH TODAY
The church needs help. When we look around at what is before us, we may look in poor shape, worn-out, and even chopped-down! The situation is not unlike what the prophet Isaiah saw. A tree stump with a bleak future!

## CLOSING CHURCHES
I once met someone from a particular denomination whose main job was to give small rural churches a good funeral. He arrived in an area with one purpose, to gently encourage small congregations that it was time to close their doors! It was intensely pastoral, as his presence was very supportive, to help them reach the conclusion, that it was alright to switch off the life support machine, and come to closure. But still – what a job!

Another time, I sat and endured a very bleak analysis in the form of a lecture from a senior leader of another denomination, whose basic conclusion was that the church across every denomination in the UK was in rapid decline. He considered that the few larger congregations which existed were insufficient to provide us with any hope that the general trend of decline could be halted. No green shoots were visible in his analysis.

## A GREEN SHOOT
However, when Isaiah continued to look at his vision of the stump of a tree, a green shoot did come up – a branch bearing good fruit.

This was an unexpected and surprising development. All seemed to be over and finished, didn't it? Hope had gone. The tree had been taken away and chopped up. What was there left to see?

But this is so typical of God. We think we have comprehended the whole, bleak picture and then suddenly, a green shoot comes up!

## NOT AS DEAD AS SUPPOSED

*'Reports of the death of the church have been greatly exaggerated'* - to misquote someone who once found himself reading his own obituary over breakfast in a national newspaper! We have no business to be writing bleak obituaries about the church. We can face facts, but stay in faith that God is with us, and that the church does have a future. It was the power of God that raised Jesus from the dead. When all *is* dead, not just having the appearance of death, even then it's not the end

of the story! When things look completely hopeless, along comes the resurrection!

## BEYOND THE IMMEDIATE

Isaiah's vision is a hopeful one. Beyond the immediate bleak appearance, there are green shoots coming! God is helping His church in ways we may not have expected. We believe that the presence of apostles in the church is part of that help. They are an important building block that God wants us to welcome and embrace, in what He has planned for the future of His church.

**This book aims to unpack what apostles look like, and how they might help all of us to be more apostolic, and grow into a vigorous and fruitful, life-giving church.**

There are four parts to this book which highlight how apostles are helping us to be apostolic.

### SENT

Our sense of purpose – the way we are positioned and handle power in dependency, our vulnerability and relationship with God, and our calling and areas of operation.

### PARENTING

How we grow up and mature as 'parents' ourselves with Father's love for those around us.

### BUILDING

How we relate and build up one another in our normal, ordinary lives – connecting, communicating, encouraging and supporting, disturbing and disrupting, and working with others as a team.

### PRESENTING

The final outcome when we are presented as a beautiful, holy Bride of Christ, in a deep communion of relationships with God and one another.

# PART ONE
# SENT

How apostles help us to understand our sense of purpose –
the way we are positioned and handle power in dependency,
our vulnerability and relationship with God, and our calling
and areas of operation.

# Heart Perfume

# Heart Perfume

Fully participate

In giving myself

In worship

This is how I was created;

Shaped with a desire to pour forth

My whole being

In selfless praise;

Thanking my God and Saviour

For His unending love;

Love which continues

Constant all the way through!

My heart bursts forth today,

To grow and blossom

A flower,

Vibrant and glowing

So happy to be picked

And held, in the hand

Of the One,

Who gave His life

For me.

*"Our lives are a Christ-like **SCENT an aroma/perfume** rising up
to God…"* 2 Corinthians 2:15

Mary Bain August 2016

# CHAPTER ONE
## 'SENTNESS'

*This word, 'sentness' that we have coined in the title of this book, seems to aptly describe the primary characteristic, which we believe apostles impart to the church. They give us a sense of purpose and direction.*

*Gifts from on high - First of all, apostles - Umbrella anointings - An atmosphere of influence - The influence of the first apostles - No super-apostles - Ordinary packaging - The basic definition - An apostle of Christ - Sent by the will of God - An aroma of sentness*

## GIFTS FROM ON HIGH

There are five gifts listed in Ephesians which are sometimes called the Ascension gifts; apostles, prophets, evangelists, pastors and teachers. They are called this, because Christ gave them to us at his Ascension. *'When he ascended on high, he led captives in his train and gave gifts to men'* (Eph.4:8). Apostles are in the list, together with the other gifts, to equip the saints for works of service so that the whole church can grow into full maturity (Eph.4:11).

## FIRST OF ALL, APOSTLES

There are many gifts God gives to the church, in fact as many as every believer that has ever lived, because we all carry within us a unique mix of them, and a way of walking in them. However these are the five listed here, and in a further list, Paul underlined the importance of three of them. He wrote, *'in the church, God has appointed first of all apostles, second prophets, third teachers...'* (1 Cor.12:28). Apostles and prophets get an even bigger heads up when Paul writes that God's household is *'built on the foundation of the apostles and prophets, with Christ Jesus himself as the chief cornerstone'* (Eph.2:20).

Apostles have something important to impart to us that is distinctive from the other Ascension gifts. All are helping to equip the church, and it is important not to bull up one gift at the expense of another. However, this book is particularly looking at how apostles help us; and they are at the top of every list we've just quoted. This suggests that they should be first of all in our thinking.

# UMBRELLA ANOINTINGS

Mary and I once attended a course which, as an illustration of the different giftings people may carry, asked some of us to stand at the front, with huge, open golf umbrellas. The idea was that we all carry a particular anointing of gifts from God, which are there for the benefit of others. As Paul writes, *'To each one the manifestation of the Spirit is given for the common good'* (1 Cor.12:7). People were invited to stand under the umbrellas of the people at the front, and ask God to use that person's anointing in their life, as a good influence.

## AN ATMOSPHERE OF INFLUENCE

The presence of the five Ascension gifts in our lives, will influence us for good in different ways, if we are open enough to receive from them. We can choose to come under their 'umbrella,' and ask God to use their anointing in our lives. When an evangelist is around people, they may become more evangelistic. His influence creates an atmosphere, or culture of evangelism, which helps the church. Likewise, apostles will help people become more apostolic. Their influence creates an apostolic atmosphere, or culture. So what might that look like? How might the presence of apostles in our lives influence us?

## THE INFLUENCE OF THE FIRST APOSTLES

The ancient Nicene Creed has the line, 'We believe in one, holy, catholic and *apostolic* church' – it acknowledges that the church is what it is, because of the anointing that the first apostles carried. Their influence goes on; their witness to the resurrection, and their Holy Spirit, inspired teaching, have been passed on for our benefit. We are still influenced by what they did two thousand years ago.

If we don't believe that apostles exist today then our openness to come under their influence will be hindered.

We believe there are apostles in the church today, just as there are all the other Ascension gifts. Their presence is bringing an apostolic influence to the church, even as the other gifts bring theirs, and as the first apostles still do.

So how do apostles influence us today? Where are they, and what do they look like?

## NO SUPER-APOSTLES

There is a lot of fog and confusion over apostles. Some deny they exist entirely – 'nothing to see here'. Alternatively, others have such a 'high view' that they define them out of any real existence. They describe an impossible super-saint, who is beyond anyone we could ever recognise! Paul himself had a word or two to say about 'super-apostles'; they didn't impress him, because he recognised the unreality and falseness of the image that was being projected (cf. 2 Cor.11:1-15). If we hide behind wrong definitions, we will miss where apostles can be found, and limit their help to us.

## ORDINARY PACKAGING

The church needs apostles but they come in ordinary human packaging, both men and women, without the glowing aura of a super-saint. They are all around us; normal people without any pretensions or airs about them. Amid all the confusion of definition, they have been trying to understand who they are, and how to get on with the work to which they feel called.

## THE BASIC DEFINITION

When things don't seem clear, we have found it is always helpful to go back to the basics.

The basic definition of the Greek word, '*apostolos*', translated, *apostle,* means simply, **'*a sent one*'.**

**If you have been sent by someone, with their authority to do something, as if they themselves were present, then you are their apostle.**

The Philippian church, for example, sent Epaphroditus to Paul as *'their apostle'* (Phil.2:25). They sent him with their full authority and backing, to be exactly what they would have been, if they had been there themselves. They sent him to look after Paul – this was the mission they had given him to fulfill. To avoid confusion and soften the meaning, in other contexts like this, *'apostolos'* is often just translated, *'messenger'* or *'representative'*.

## AN APOSTLE OF CHRIST
While all 'apostles' are sent by someone, we are especially looking at the ones sent by God. More accurately, apostles are particularly sent by Christ. This is what Paul often stated at the start of his letters, *'Paul, an apostle of Christ'*.

However, there are exceptions - in the letter to the Galatians, Paul wrote that both Christ and God the Father had sent him, so we shouldn't get too pedantic (Gal.1:1). Even the Holy Spirit can claim to send apostles, because at Antioch, He is described as setting apart Paul and Barnabas, as apostles, for their first mission trip (Acts 13:1-3, 14:4).

The Trinity may all be involved in sending apostles, but they are still particularly sent by Christ. They go, especially, with his authority, because they are one with him, just as the members of a human body are one with the head of the body.

## SENT BY THE WILL OF GOD
*'Paul, called to be an apostle of Christ Jesus by the will of God...'.* This description at the start of Paul's letter to the Corinthians, is typical of how he sees himself (1 Cor.1:1).

Like Paul, today's apostles have been called and sent on assignment by the will of God. Later, we will be looking at how apostles help to establish the Kingdom of God in other ways, but this sense of being sent by God's will, ('sentness'), describes the foundational influence they have upon us. Through the influence of apostles, we discover that, like them, we are all on assignment.

## AN AROMA OF SENTNESS

As 'sent ones', apostles impart an aroma of 'sentness' to the church. An apostolic atmosphere in a church will fill it with the scent of 'sentness'! Their influence wakes us up; and we become aware of, and released into, our calling and purpose in God. Their presence re-aligns us with who we are in Christ, and with the assignments in life to which we are called. It is a perfume with which the Lord is really pleased.

This is why apostles are foundational – they wake us up to our destiny. Teachers teach us, pastors care for us, evangelists share the good news that we can be forgiven and saved, prophets comfort and encourage us, but it is apostles that wake us up to God's direction and purpose for our lives.

However, with the awakening of purpose, we need to understand our dependency on God in order to fulfill it. Apostles can help us with this lesson too.

*'Bloom where you are planted; you can be SCENT where you are'*

*(Arthur Burt)*

# CHAPTER TWO
# POWER AND DEPENDENCY

*Apostles are sent out in power __and__ dependency. If we look at the detail of how Jesus sent out the Twelve and then later, the Seventy-two, we see how he wanted the apostles to always recognise their dependency on him. This lesson is summarised in Jesus words, 'apart from me you can do nothing' (Jn.15:5) - we are entirely dependent on him in everything.*

*A lesson for the twelve - A lesson over a meal - A lesson in a boat - The seventy-two - Little children - Little flock - Sent in powerful vulnerability - A herd of bulls - Lambs among wolves - Reliance on others - Received or rejected - Yoked oxen - Meek nobility - Washing feet*

## A LESSON FOR THE TWELVE

In the gospels we read how Jesus sent out his twelve disciples in twos on their first mission trip, calling them 'apostles', because they were *'sent ones'*, (Mk.3:14-15). When they returned, they reported back to Jesus all the amazing things that *they* had done and taught. Demons had been driven out of people, and many healings had taken place. They had laid hands on the sick and anointed them with oil in the name of Jesus (Mk.6:13). It was clear that although they had gone without him, when they encountered evil, they had dealt with it, as if Jesus had been there.

This time, the Twelve had not just been messengers, carrying a message that Jesus was on the way, although he did sometimes send them ahead to do this (Lk.9:52). But this was completely different - the Twelve had done the business! It must have been a heady experience - a perfect storm for an argument on who might be the greatest!

Jesus decides to take them to a quiet place to be alone. Mark's gospel records him saying, *'Come with me by yourselves to a quiet place and get some rest'* (Mk.6:31). They needed to get away from all the buzz of what had gone on, re-adjust and remember that they were still dependent on him. Unfortunately, the crowds followed them, and so they had to learn more about dependency in the noise of the crowd; and later on, in a storm at sea rather than on a quiet retreat!

## A LESSON OVER A MEAL

Later the same day, the crowd needed feeding and Jesus turned to the Twelve and said, *'You give them something to eat'*. Without his help, they knew that there was no way that they could feed anyone! They looked at the circumstances through rational eyes and saw that it was impossible. Where was food to be purchased anyway, for this number of people, even if they had the money? All they could suggest was to send the crowd away.

But then, of course, the miracle occurred; and the Twelve took five loaves of bread out of Jesus' hands and distributed them among five thousand people. The bread had multiplied in *their* hands but the miracle had come through Jesus. The apostles' power to do anything miraculous was entirely dependent on Him.

## A LESSON IN A BOAT

After the miracle, Jesus dismissed the crowd, while he went off alone up a mountain. In Mark's gospel, chapter six, it says that he *insisted* that the Twelve crossed the lake without him (Mk.6:45). They didn't know it, but they were about to begin a very long night. The wind was against them and the waves grew rough, and after hours of rowing, they were not getting anywhere fast. Meanwhile Jesus was seeing it all from a mountaintop and just waited (Mk.6:48)!

At the fourth watch of the night, a long time later, Jesus started out towards them, walking on the water. The experience of rowing through the night, but getting nowhere, was how the Twelve would realise their dependency on him, and how inadequate they were in their own strength. Immediately, as Jesus got into the boat, the wind died down, and they reached the shore, towards which they had been heading (Jn.6:21). The presence of Jesus made all the difference.

What I find amazing is that Jesus gave the disciples the opportunity to decide whether they wanted him on board or not! Mark records that he was going to walk on by them (Mk.6:48). The Twelve had to positively decide to receive him into the boat.

Peter also had a further lesson in dependency, when he stepped out of the boat to walk on the water towards Jesus. While his eyes were fixed on Jesus, all was well, but as soon as he looked elsewhere, he began to sink, and Jesus had to hold out his hand to rescue him (Mt.14:29-30).

## THE SEVENTY-TWO

Another group, this time of seventy-two, were sent out later with the same power and authority as the Twelve. They also returned rejoicing, at the amazing things that they had done, saying, *'Lord, even the demons submit to us in your name'* (Lk.10:17). But Jesus realigned their thinking and described them as *'little children'*, telling them to rejoice rather that their names were written in heaven (Lk.10:20).

## LITTLE CHILDREN

*'Little children'* is a term of endearment and relationship, but at the same time, it would have re-framed who they were, in

terms of their dependency. The success which the Seventy-two had experienced was not something they had achieved of themselves. Theirs was a given authority. They were just 'little children'. The things that were happening around them, and through them, had been hidden from the wise and learned, but revealed to them as little children, because it was their Father in Heaven's good pleasure to do so (Lk.10:21). The Father had revealed these things to Jesus, and he, in turn, had chosen to reveal these things to them (Lk.10:22). Their situation was one of entire dependency on God, through Jesus.

## LITTLE FLOCK

The same message of dependency is seen in Luke's gospel, chapter twelve; Jesus warned the disciples to expect trouble (Lk.12:11) but then reassured them, *'Fear not, little flock, for it is your Father's good pleasure to give you the Kingdom'* (Lk.12:32). So despite the fact that God is giving them a Kingdom, he calls them a *'little flock'*. Jesus was their shepherd and they were a *'little flock'* dependent on him to lead them (Jn.10:11, 14).

## SENT IN POWERFUL VULNERABILITY

Now here is the odd, upside down thing about the Kingdom of God. We have power on the one hand and vulnerability on the other.

The Twelve had been given all the power and authority of Jesus to wreak destructive, unstoppable havoc on the kingdom of darkness and oppression. Their healing of the sick, raising of the dead, cleansing of lepers, and driving out of demons, all proclaimed and established that the Kingdom rule of God had arrived (Mt.10:7-8).

## A HERD OF BULLS

One of our apostle friends felt God had described apostles to him, as a herd of bulls. The Twelve were the proverbial 'bull in a china shop'; Satan, being totally helpless and unable to stop the plundering of his stolen goods. It was the same for the Seventy-two. They had trampled on *'snakes and scorpions and overcome all the power of the enemy* (Lk.10:18-19). No power of the enemy could withstand them. This was indeed taking the territory by force! *'From the days of John the Baptist until now, the kingdom of heaven has been forcefully advancing, and <u>forceful men</u> lay hold of it'* (Mt.11:12). They were taking the territory boldly and courageously. Like Joshua, taking the Promised Land, they were being *'strong and courageous'* (Josh.1:9).

## LAMBS AMONG WOLVES

Yet, amazingly, at the same time, both the Twelve and the

Seventy-two were sent out in complete weakness and vulnerability, to the people they were to encounter. *'I am sending you out like sheep among wolves'*, Jesus says to the Twelve (Mt.10:16). *'...like lambs among wolves'*, he says to the Seventy-two (Lk.10:3).

Previously, Jesus had looked at the crowds with compassion, describing them as harassed and helpless, and in need of a shepherd (Mt. 9:36). He had then sent out his apostles with his power and authority to find *'the lost sheep of Israel'* (Mt.10:6). But he sent them, not as shepherds but as sheep, themselves! Also, without Jesus their shepherd physically with them, they really were lambs among wolves!

## RELIANCE ON OTHERS

Jesus' instructions, as he sent out his apostles, reinforced this vulnerability. They were not to be self-reliant, but to rely on others. *'Do not take along any gold or silver or copper in your belts; take no bag for the journey, or extra tunic, or sandals or a staff'* (Mt.10:9-10). He told them that, as they went from village to village, 'men of peace' would welcome them into their homes, and look after them (Lk.10:5-7).

When he gives details of their dependency upon others for even a cup of cold water, again Jesus describes the apostles in vulnerable terms, as *'little ones'* ( see Mt.10:42),

## RECEIVED OR REJECTED

These 'forceful men' who were advancing the kingdom against the enemy, were being taught by Jesus to have a very different approach towards the people they were meeting. They might be rejected, as well as received by them. They would face opposition and persecution as well as good receptions. The apostles' experience of power and authority was going to be very different to that of the world.

As they were sent out, Jesus reminds them of their intimate connection with Himself, as His apostles. *'He who listens to you, listens to me; he who rejects you, rejects me; but he who rejects me, rejects him who sent me'* (Lk.10:16). He was the one sending them out, and they were going in the same manner as Jesus went. Just like Him, they might be listened to, or they might be rejected.

## YOKED OXEN

*'A student is not above his teacher, nor a servant above his master. It is enough for the student to be like his teacher, and the servant like his master'* (Mt.10:24-25). *'... but everyone who is fully trained will be like his teacher'* (Lk.6:40).

Jesus wanted his apostles to learn from him, and to be meek and lowly in heart – *'Take my yoke upon you and learn from me'* Jesus says (Mt.11:29).

These 'bulls' that were overcoming the evil one, were also learning to be meek and lowly oxen, gently and obediently yoked together, and responsive to whatever direction in which God wanted them to go. That is the definition for meekness, from the underlying Greek word, *'praus'*. Jesus was asking them to lay down the pride of life, and to be completely under his direction and leading.

## MEEK NOBILITY

In the natural, farmers will neuter bulls, in order to make them less aggressive. Then, as oxen, they can utilise all their strength in ploughing the soil, and bringing in the harvest. What a wonder, to which the apostles were being called, to take all the nobility of being children of God, and to assume willingly instead the meek, servant role of an ox!

Jesus had said the harvest was plentiful but the labourers were few. He had then told them to ask the Lord of the harvest to send out harvest workers into the harvest. By the next day, they were the ones on the launch pad, being released as apostles into the harvest field! They had become the answer to their own prayer.

The oxen were needed for the harvest. *'Where there are no oxen the manger is empty but from the strength of an ox comes an abundant harvest'* (Prov.14:4). The power and authority that the apostles held as children of God, was needed now, as harvest workers. The apostles were not being forced to be oxen, but to willingly volunteer to put their heads under the yoke and follow Jesus into the harvest.

## WASHING FEET

Jesus had set them an example. *'The Son of man did not come to be served but to serve'* (Mt.20:28). Later, at the last supper, he

spelt it out yet again, when he washed the disciple's feet. '*...
Now that I, your Lord and Teacher, have washed your feet, you also
should wash one another's feet...I tell you the truth, no servant is
greater than his master, nor is an apostle greater than the one who
sent him*' (Jn.13:13-16).

The greatest in God's kingdom was in fact to become a slave
of all (Mk.10:44). Jesus points out that this is the very opposite
of the world's understanding of authority and greatness. '*You
know that the rulers of the gentiles lord it over them, and their high
officials exercise authority over them. Not so with you*' (Mt.20:25-
26).

The apostles show us how to handle power, with humility and
dependence upon God. However, Jesus also sent out His
apostles with His authority. We can learn a lesson from their
experience in this too.

# CHAPTER THREE
## AUTHORITY
## AND RELATIONSHIP

*Apostles are sent with authority, but what in practice does this mean? There is a lesson for us to learn, that we are all sent with authority; and our exercise of it grows, as our relationship with God grows.*

*The authority of Jesus - A growing understanding - An intimate relationship - The authority of the apostles - Friendship with Jesus - The presence of the Spirit - The extension of the mission - Signs and wonders*

## THE AUTHORITY OF JESUS

When Jesus says *'All authority in heaven and earth has been given to me'* he meant it (Mt.28:18). Jesus knew he'd been sent by His Father with all His authority. This was his understanding of himself as an apostle – *'a sent one'*. He constantly referred to himself as, *'the One whom God has sent'*. The letter to the Hebrews even describes Jesus as an apostle (Heb.3:1).

## A GROWING UNDERSTANDING

The Father sent His Son into the world in order to save the world, and so, Jesus became a baby, and grew up. Year by year, he went through a growing understanding of his mission. As a baby, he knew nothing, but at the age of twelve, he was saying to his earthly parents that God was his Father; and astonishing the teachers of the law, in the Temple, with his difficult questions (Lk.2:46-47). At the age of thirty, he was declaring to his disciples that he only did what he saw his Father doing (Jn. 5:19); that he only spoke the words his Father was speaking (Jn.3:34, 8:28); that his food was to do the will of the One who had sent him (Jn.4:34); and that he and his Father were one (Jn.17:22). Jesus bluntly gave this summary statement to his disciples, *'If you have seen me, you have seen the Father'* (Jn.14:9). Jesus knew who he was!

## AN INITIMATE RELATIONSHIP

Throughout John's gospel, an intimate relationship is portrayed between the Father and the Son. There is a deep love and unity displayed between them. Jesus constantly spent time in His Father's company. He knew what God wanted him to do, because he was constantly with Him, talking and listening to Him. So when we read of the amazing miracles and teaching of Jesus, we understand that they are a direct result of the intimate relationship he had with his Father. He was doing on earth, the will of his Father, because as His Son, he understood intimately what that will was.

## THE AUTHORITY OF THE APOSTLES

In a similar way, Jesus saw his first apostles as 'sent ones', sent by him, with the same power and authority with which he, himself, had been sent by his Father.

In John, chapter seventeen, Jesus prayed to his Father, and said, *'As you sent me into the world, I have sent them into the world'* (Jn.17:18). He said to them after his resurrection, *'As the Father has sent me, I am sending you'* (Jn.20:21). During the last supper, he told them, *'I tell you the truth, no servant is greater than his master, nor is an apostle greater than the one who sent him'* (Jn.13:16). They were his apostles even as he was His Father's apostle.

When the Father said to Jesus, 'You are My Son', He was saying that whatever you do is being done in My name, and My authority. This is exactly the same as what Jesus was saying to his apostles as he sent them out. The disciples were one with Jesus, just as Jesus was one with the Father. Their apostleship was subsumed within his. So whatever the apostles did was being done in the name of Jesus, and with his authority.

## FRIENDSHIP WITH JESUS

When Jesus selected the twelve apostles, Mark's gospel emphasises that they were to spend their lives with him - *'He appointed the twelve...that they might be <u>with him</u> and that he might send them out to preach and to have authority to drive out demons'* (Mk.3:14-15). In other words, they were being invited into intimacy and friendship *with him*. He said to them later, *'I no longer call you servants, I call you friends'* (Jn.15:15)

Just as Jesus and the Father were one, Jesus wanted his apostles to be one with him. In order for this to happen, they needed to stay close to him. When we hang around someone, we get to understand what they are like. We are tuned into their thinking, and even start to imitate their way of speaking and doing things.

## THE PRESENCE OF THE SPIRIT

In Acts, chapter four, Peter and John spoke boldly about Jesus while the Sanhedrin listened in astonishment. They noted that these uneducated, ordinary men had been *with Jesus* (Acts 4:13). However, a wonderful transformation had taken place, since the Twelve had first known him. The Holy Spirit had been given to them. They were now speaking with a new boldness, coming from his presence within them. Beforehand, the Spirit had been with them, but now he was in them (Jn.14:17). This was the Spirit who Jesus had said would teach them what to say, and how to say it, who would take from what was his, and reveal it to them (Jn.16:13-15).

The presence of the Spirit within the apostles, took them to a new level of closeness with Jesus, which they had never previously experienced, even when they'd lived and walked with him through his teaching ministry. Jesus had said to them, before his death, *'It is* <u>*better*</u> *that I go away, then the Spirit will come'* (Jn.16:7). The Holy Spirit was described by Jesus as *'another Helper'* (Jn.14:16). The use of the Greek word, *allos*, in this phrase means that a fuller translation is:- *'another Helper of the* <u>*same kind*</u> *as I have been'*. The apostles could continue to be *with Jesus*, knowing a closeness of relationship with him, because his Spirit had come to live inside them.

## THE EXTENSION OF THE MISSION

In John, chapter seventeen, Jesus says, *'I have given them the glory that you gave me, that they may be one, as we are one'* (Jn.17:22). We referenced this earlier in the chapter, to show that the Father and the Son were one in their mission. Now we read in this same passage, that the oneness of their mission is being extended, not only to include the first apostles, but also to all who would believe their message, as well. *'My prayer is not for them alone. I pray also for those who will believe in me through their message that all of them may be one...'* (Jn.17:20-21). All of us are one in the same mission, *'that the world may believe...'* (Jn.17:21).

We may not have realised it, but the harvest field is all around us! It hasn't gone away since the first apostles were sent out. Jesus, in his compassion for the crowds, is still asking us to pray to the Lord of the harvest, for harvest workers to be sent out into the fields. Jesus is still telling us to *'open [our] eyes and look at the fields. They are ripe for harvest'* (John 4:35). As Paul wrote, *'Now is the day of salvation'* (2 Cor.6:2). There are crowds who are ready now, just waiting to be harvested. We too have a sickle, which we need to pick up and use, to bring in the harvest. We all have a job to do!

However, just like the first apostles, our relationship with Jesus is vital. We cannot be successful in anything we do without him. It is only through friendship with Jesus that we can understand what he wants, and are able to be sent out with his authority.

## SIGNS AND WONDERS

Apostles, sent in the authority of Jesus, establish the Kingdom of God through signs and wonders, with the driving out of the demonic and the healing of the sick!

This was the instruction of Jesus to His first apostles; to the Twelve, *'to heal the sick, cleanse lepers, raise the dead, cast out demons'* (Mt.10:7-8), and then, to the Seventy-two, *'Heal the sick and say, the kingdom of God has come near you'* (Lk.10:9). Later, Paul wrote of his own experience that *'the things that mark an apostle – signs, wonders and miracles- were done among you...'* (2 Cor.12:12). He wrote that people had come *'to obey God by what I have said and done – by the power of signs and miracles through the power of the Spirit...'* (Rom.15:18-19).

However, we must not think that signs and wonders are exclusive to apostles. It should be no surprise to see them being done by every believer, since Jesus has extended the invitation, for us all to be sent on mission. So we read at the end of Mark's gospel, *'These signs will <u>accompany those who believe</u>: in my name they will drive out demons...they will place hands on the sick, and they will get well'* (Mk.16:18). If we are a believer, then we can expect signs and wonders to accompany us too.

As we proclaim the gospel, signs and wonders may happen through us, but only in the context of our friendship with Jesus. Like the first apostles, we are sent with an authority based on our relationship with God. This is why, we are told to pray, *'Your Kingdom come, Your Will be done on earth as it is in heaven'*. Our prayer life with God matters! Through our prayers, what was out of order comes into line with God's purposes, and we see the Kingdom of God on earth as it is in Heaven.

We are all one in this mission, on which Jesus has sent out his apostles. As we stay close to God and are open to learn from the apostles around us, then we will grow in exercising the authority that God has given to all of us.

.

# CHAPTER FOUR
## NEEDED

*Apostles find us and release us into the harvest field. They tell us that we, too, are needed.*

*Donkeys on a big mission - Found and released - Responding to opposition - Reminded of our mission*

Like in the Oxford and Cambridge boat races, we are not here just to be spectators, while a few specialist people row the boat. We are the ones in the boat, manning the oars!

No-one is unnecessary in the body of Jesus. We cannot say that we are not needed (1 Cor.12:21). God has sent us all out into the harvest. He has called us His fellow workers, and we are partners with Him in the proclaiming of the gospel (2 Cor.6:1). He has made us His ambassadors, making His appeal through us (2 Cor.5:20), that *'God our Saviour wants all men to be saved and to come to the knowledge of the truth'* (1Tim 2:3-4).

## DONKEYS ON A BIG MISSION

One word which the Lord gave to Mary and I, as we headed off to Bible college, was that we were *'two donkeys that the Lord had need of!'* It doesn't sound too wonderful, does it, to be described as a donkey? However, the Lord spoke to us, very clearly, through that bit of the gospel story, where Jesus is about to ride into Jerusalem on the back of a young donkey. The donkey, along with its mother, was carrying the presence of Jesus into the city, into the heart of the temple, where he would put everything into order; driving out the den of robbers, and establishing it as a House of prayer for all nations. Put like that, the donkeys were on a big, important mission after all!

Mary and I have always felt happy to be called *'two donkeys the Lord has need of'*. We have understood that we have an important mission, to bring the presence of Jesus into people's lives, and this has encouraged us, many times as we have entered new places and situations, over the years.

## FOUND AND RELEASED

If you go to the story in Matthew, chapter twenty-one, you can read that two disciples were sent to get the donkeys. Jesus told the disciples exactly where to find them, and that they were to untie them and bring them back to him (Mt.21:1-2). This is a wonderful picture of how apostles are used to release people into their purpose and mission.

Apostles, directed by Jesus, may come into our lives, to seek us out and release us into the job he wants us to do. We may have got ourselves into a complete mess, tied up and in the wrong place, but Jesus really does know how to find us and get us back on track! In our own case, when we first heard this 'donkey' word, we felt that God was releasing us, with His blessing, from our occupations and location, so that we could go off to Bible College.

## RESPONDING TO OPPOSITION

When the disciples were untying the donkeys, they were challenged, not only by the people hanging around, but even by the donkey's owners, *'What are you doing, untying that colt?'* (Lk.19:33, Mk.11:5-6). As a picture of what may happen when we are released to be of service to the Lord, it is a warning that we should expect opposition.

However, Jesus had told his disciples ahead of time, that there would be protests, and what answer they should give when it happened – *'the Lord needs them'* (Mt.21:3).
How reassuring it is to know that the Lord has need of us!

Apostles wake us up, with these words, *'the Lord has need of you'*. We may have felt irrelevant, but God's word says otherwise! The Body of Jesus is made up of many parts; each part must do its work (Eph.4:16), and every part is needed. The most unconnected people, standing idly around in your lives, may suddenly have an opinion about what you are doing, as well as close friends and family; and try to prevent or delay you. Obviously the devil doesn't want us to be released into God's calling for our lives, and will also do his worst to stop us! Just remember – *'the Lord has need of you!'*

## REMINDED OF OUR MISSION

Apostles remind us of our mission, who we are, and why we are here. If we have been feeling directionless, they get us back to the point, and untie and release us. They remind us, for example, from the parable in Matthew, chapter twenty, that the farmer has come again into the market place to hire more workers.

We hear his question, in the parable, with a new clarity, *'Why have you been standing here all day long doing nothing?'* (Mt.20:6). To the reply, *'no-one has hired us'*, we hear the farmer say, *'You also, go'* (Mt.20:7) – *'the Lord has need of you'*.

# The Missing Piece

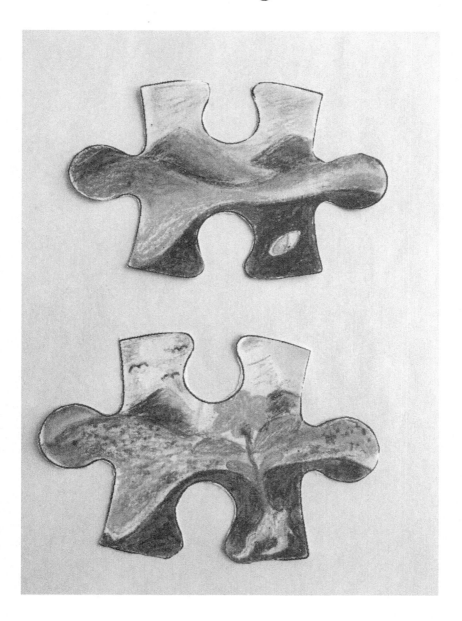

# The Missing Piece
(Inspired by an episode from The Chosen TV Channel)

God needs me to serve Him
If I do not do it, no one else will.
There will be a gap!
There is a place in His heart, His plan,
That has my shape in it.
I am chosen to do my part
To be who He has called me to be.
I am part of the jigsaw,
And so are you.
Not just believers,
But those who are not yet believers too!
There is a place for all of us;
That is why we must find others,
Tell them to "Come and see;
While there is still time
To complete the jigsaw."

We are all needed!
Find your place,
His heart is aching for you. Yes, you!
You are the piece He is missing!
Being that piece,
Coming to Him and laying down,
You will find the <u>peace</u>
That you have been missing.
You will know, that all along
You have always been in His heart;
So special to Him!
Chosen to be with Him,
Chosen to be loved,
Chosen to serve.

(See Mark 10:45; Mark 3:14; John 1:45,46)          Mary Bain  April 2021

# CHAPTER FIVE
## CALLING

*There is a way chosen for us by God in which He promises to guide us (Ps.25:12).*

*'Not me, lord!' - Something more - 'I am has sent me' - A Cyrus mission - God's appointment - Declaring the move – Rebuilding - Subduing opposition - Breaking through barriers -Given hidden treasures - Finding direction*

The psalmist wrote, *'All the days ordained for me were written in your book before one of them came to be'* (Ps.139:16). Our lives truly are in God's hands – He has called us, and fashioned us, for things only we can do. There are *'...good works which God prepared in advance for us to do'* (Eph.2:10). No-one can change God's calling on their lives. God is the one who calls, and He is at the beginning and the end of the process, and all the way through the middle as well.

### 'NOT ME, LORD!'
Moses was called by God to rescue the people of Israel and bring them into the land which He had promised them. This didn't stop him arguing with God that he wasn't really the right choice. *'What if they don't believe me or listen to me...?'* (Ex.4:1). God reassured him that He would demonstrate His power, through the staff in Moses' hand.

Moses then complained, *'O Lord, I have never been eloquent...I am slow of speech and tongue'* (Ex.4:10). Again, God reassured him, *'I will help you speak and will teach you what to say'* (Ex.4:12). Finally, Moses said, *'O Lord, please send someone else to do it'* (Ex.4:13). However, God gave him Aaron, his brother, to help him; and Moses, who had run out of any further arguments, sets off on the adventure of his life!

We may feel that God has got it wrong regarding the calling on our own lives, but of course, He hasn't. Who can win an argument with Him? He takes us on a process and is willing to talk through our worries and objections. There may be years of preparation, but God understands what He is doing, and has not forgotten the bigger picture, even if we may have contented ourselves with something less.

## SOMETHING MORE

When I was baptised, someone gave me a prophetic word, which has often helped me. He said that I would keep coming up to a ceiling, and say, 'Is this it, Lord?', and the reply back would be, 'No, there's a hole in this ceiling – climb through!'

This word is really about the 'something more', that God has for us at every stage of our lives. There are no dead ends; no brick walls with Him – there is always a way through. We mustn't go to sleep, or stay put, when we should be moving into new things. *'Since we live by the Spirit, let us keep in step with the Spirit'* (Gal.5:25). If God is moving, then it is time for us to step out too! If the way seems unclear, and doors look firmly shut, wait expectantly. I recently saw a picture of a hallway, with a door at the end of it – the caption said, *'Until the Lord opens the next door, praise Him in the hallway'*. This is a great attitude to have! Keep sensitive to God's pace for your life, and praise Him in every circumstance. If there is breath in your body, you can be sure that He has something more for you to move into.

## 'I AM HAS SENT ME'

In Exodus, chapter three, we can see God using the 'sent' language of an apostle in His calling of Moses. As we read on,

we notice how often Moses is referred to, as a man *'sent'* from God. The ancient Greek translation, (the Septuagint), even translates the Hebrew using the verb form of *'apostolos'* – (the word translated *'sent'* in English). Moses was being called to be God's apostle to the people of Israel. His mission was to release them from bondage and re-position them into God's plans and purposes. He was to take them out of Egypt and into the Promised Land. As an apostle, the first words the people of Israel heard Moses speak were, *'I AM has <u>sent</u> me to you'* (Ex.3:14).

Whatever it is that we sense God is calling us to do, our confidence, in doing it, has to be founded on those words, *'I AM has sent me'*. We needn't be falsely modest or proud; we are who we are, because God has got hold of us, and made us so. Paul wrote about being the least of the apostles, not even deserving to be one, but he then concluded with the words, *'By the grace of God I am what I am, and his grace to me was not without effect...'* (1 Cor.15:10).

We are who we are – we do not need to apologise for it. Whatever our calling, it is a call from God; and His grace will work within us, to fulfil it.

## A CYRUS MISSION

Not all callings are as dramatic as that of Moses. We may just have a growing awareness of who we are and what God has called us to do. Sometimes the different things, we feel that God has said to us, come together, and begin to make sense. It's like He has been showing us first one side, and then another, of a beautifully shaped object, so that finally, we understand the bigger perspective.

God may tell us things way ahead of time, so that we may feel puzzled as to what it all means. This happened to me one day while I was sitting in my car, stuck in a traffic jam. As I sat there, I looked across the road at a shop selling electrical goods, and right across the window, on a big diagonal poster, were the words, 'Cyrus Mission'. What an odd choice of name for a piece of electrical equipment, I thought! But as I took in the words, I felt God say to me, *'This is what you are on - a Cyrus mission'*. Now, Cyrus played a crucial role in the history of the people of Israel; being instrumental in their return from exile. In contrast, I was leading one of the smaller churches, in a small city, in the UK – this word hardly seemed to fit with my circumstances. However, I received it, as a declaration that despite my misgivings, there was something about my mission that was akin to that of Cyrus. I didn't share this with anyone at the time. What was the point! I felt deep inside that it would only make real sense to me later.

I believe that God sometimes gives words like this one, early on in our Christian life, so that we have time to ponder on them. Then, later, they can reassure us about the direction on which we have been travelling. They help us to understand our characters and our calling.

## GOD'S APPOINTMENT

We can certainly learn something from God's calling of Cyrus. In the first year of his reign as King of Persia, God used him to bring the people of Israel back from exile into Jerusalem. Cyrus decreed, *'The Lord…has **appointed** me to build a temple for him at Jerusalem…Anyone of His people among you -…let him go* *up'* (2 Ch.36:23). This decree from King Cyrus allowed God's people to come home, to their own land.

Now here is a remarkable thing - about a hundred and fifty years earlier, Cyrus was described in a passage of prophecy from Isaiah, (chapters 44 and 45), as the one who would do this; before he was even born! Isaiah sees ahead to a man whom God would call and use. *'[The LORD] who says of Cyrus, He is my shepherd, and will accomplish all that I please...'* (Isa.44:28).

He is God's **anointed**. *'This is what the LORD says to His anointed, to Cyrus, whose right hand I take hold of...'* (Isa.45:1).

God was the one who **summoned** him. *'...I am the LORD, the God of Israel who summons you [Cyrus] by name'* (Isa.45:3).

God is the one who **raised** him up. *'I will raise up Cyrus in my righteousness...'* (Isa.46:13).

It is an awesome thing to realise that, before we were ever born, God singled us out, and spoke His words over each of us, declaring who He had called *us* to be. Like Cyrus, God has appointed and anointed us, summoned and raised us up. *'For you created my inmost being; you knit me together in my mother's womb...all the days ordained for me were written in your book before one of them came to be'* (cf. Ps.139:13-16).

## DECLARING THE NEXT MOVE

In many ways, Cyrus was fulfilling a similar role to the role of an apostle. He was sent with God's authority to establish God's purposes on the earth. The first thing Cyrus did was to initiate the moving of God's people back into their proper position. In this instance, they were in Babylon, and needed to be in Jerusalem. A shift of direction was needed, and Cyrus was there to do it. This is one of the things we can learn from Cyrus, relating to the way in which apostles operate - they declare and establish the next move of God.

## REBUILDING

We can learn more about what apostles do, as we consider Isaiah's prophecies about Cyrus. *'[The LORD] who says of Jerusalem, It shall be inhabited, of the towns of Judah, They shall be built, and of their ruins, I will restore them'* (Isa.44:26).
*'...[Cyrus] will say of Jerusalem, Let it be rebuilt, and of the temple, Let its foundations be laid'* (Isa.44:28).
*'...He will rebuild my city and set my exiles free, but not for a price or reward'* (Isa.46:13).

It is clear from these verses that God called Cyrus to be a builder. Similarly, apostles are builders – they initiate and implement the new things that God is doing. They lay the foundations. They get the plumb line out, and check that the walls are being built true and straight. As Paul wrote, *'By the grace God has given me, I laid a foundation as an expert builder...'* (1 Cor.3:10).

## SUBDUING OPPOSITION

The LORD promised Cyrus that He would subdue nations before him, strip kings of their armour, and that He would go before him, and level the mountains (Isa.45:1-2). Apostles will encounter opposition, but with it, God promises that He will make a way through it all. This was the experience of the apostle Paul – he was able to write that *'a great door for effective work has opened for me __and__ there are many who oppose me'* (1 Cor.16:7). We can draw comfort in this respect when he also wrote, *'Who shall separate us from the love of Christ? Shall trouble or hardship or persecution or famine or nakedness or danger or sword? ... No in all these things we are more than conquerors through him who loved us'* (Ro.8:35, 37).

## BREAKING THROUGH BARRIERS

*'...Cyrus whose right hand I take hold of ...to open doors before him so that gates will not be shut...I will break down gates of bronze and cut through bars of iron'* (Isa 45:1-2). These are the same words used in Ps 107:16 for the release of prisoners, *'[The LORD] breaks down gates of bronze and cuts through bars of iron'*.

Apostles bring breakthrough. Where things have stalled, where people have been hung out to dry, or are in a state of paralysis, apostles affirm, release and recognise the gifting in them. They help us to come into a new freedom, shifting our thinking back to the things of God.

## GIVEN HIDDEN TREASURES

*'I will give you the treasures of darkness, riches stored in secret places...'* (Isa.45:3, concerning Cyrus). God's people are the 'hidden treasures' that apostles are given out of the darkness. When Jesus went to the cross, the great joy which he anticipated ahead of him, was all the children who would come into God's kingdom, through his death and resurrection (Heb.12:2). In a quote from Isaiah, Jesus says, *'Here I am, and the children God has given me'* (Heb.2:13).

This is what the Kingdom of God is like - Jesus describes in one parable, the joy of finding treasure, hidden in a field (Mt.13:44). I once thought heaven would be a beautiful, empty place of hills and meadows, rivers and streams. In fact, the really wonderful thing about heaven is that it is full of people – it isn't empty at all! Just as Mary and I love and treasure our children; in the same way, God loves and treasures every one of us.

## FINDING DIRECTION

*'One thing I ask of the Lord, this is what I seek; that I may dwell in the house of the Lord all the days of my life, to gaze upon the beauty of the Lord and to seek Him in His temple'* (Ps.27:4).

God is calling us into a growing love and ache for His presence. He loves our company, and when we are with Him, we cannot help but worship Him. If we stay close to God, we can sense His heartbeat, and understand the direction He wants us to go.

Recently, Mary and I were wondering what was right for us to do next. There were so many possible ways forward! We felt God tell us to set aside time with Him, in worship. We sensed that from that place of intimacy, we would get clear direction for what was ahead, not only for ourselves, but also for others in our area. So we began worshipping regularly, as a small group, over a twelve week period. We were amazed at the clarity of direction which emerged, and also our renewed confidence in God's ability to lead us.

During this special time of worship, God gave us, as a foundational word, a passage in Acts, where teachers and prophets in the church at Antioch, worshipped and fasted together; '...*While they were worshipping the Lord, and fasting, the Holy Spirit said, Set apart for me Barnabas and Saul for the work to which I have called them...*' (Acts 13:1-3). We saw that from a place of worship intimacy, they had received direction for mission. As a result of hearing this, the Antioch church sent off Paul and Barnabas on their first missionary journey. And from this point onwards, they were both described as apostles (Acts 14:14).

Our closeness to God in worship is the only place for us to safely receive direction for our lives, and to understand not only <u>what</u> He wants us to do, but also <u>where</u> He wants us to go, and to <u>which people</u>.

# CHAPTER SIX
## TERRITORY

*God gives specific assignments to each one of us, in the places where He has sent us. There is a general sense of calling, but then there is the detail of our positioning. Apostles remind us, that we are where we are for a reason. We may think we live in a place because of our job, or to be near the grandchildren, or because we were born there, but in fact, God has positioned us there.*

*Sent to the ends of the earth - No limits - Paul's sense of territory - The work done by others - New territory in the north - A bigger shift than expected - The God who opens doors – Governorship - Governing the territory with worship - Prophetic singing - Prayer walking the territory*

*'God made every nation of men ... and He determined the times set for them and the exact places where they should live'*
(Acts 17:26).

## SENT TO THE ENDS OF THE EARTH

Let's not put any limits on what God may be assigning for us to do! I once went forward in a Christian conference, responding to one of those, 'willing to go anywhere' calls for prayer. Mary and I were in the middle of major changes in our life, and were actually considering a move to New Zealand, at the time. So, as this friend was praying for me, in my head, I said to the Lord, 'New Zealand – is this where You want me to go?' Suddenly, however, I saw in large, bold, upper case letters, the word

# 'TAHITI'

hovering immediately in front of my eyes! I was amazed!

Just then, Mary came towards me, before I could return to my seat, and another friend prayed for her, as I stood nearby. I hadn't had an opportunity to share with her yet, about what had just taken place. After praying, this friend chatted with us both briefly, and then said how God can send people to all sorts of places – his own son, for example, had gone off to Tahiti. He then, immediately corrected himself, and said, 'Haiti, I meant Haiti,' but he had said it, the word, Tahiti! Over the space of a few minutes, it had come up twice! God had definitely got my attention!

During the remaining time at the camp conference, nothing else dramatic happened, but I did find myself reading passages from Isaiah, which talked about *'islands at the ends of the earth'*. I later found out that this phrase is a description that Christians in Tahiti, often apply to themselves, because the island of Tahiti is in the middle of the South Pacific Ocean, miles from anywhere!

## NO LIMITS

God was giving me unexpected direction beyond anything I could have ever dreamt up. At the start of a new season in our lives, there I was suddenly booking flights, for a visit to Tahiti! I sensed that the purpose of this visit was to show me something, rather than a directive to go and live there. In fact, it wasn't until I was flying back at the end of my visit, that two things happened; firstly I received a flood of prophetic words, centred around the idea of creating a network of 'welcome places'; and secondly, I had a huge enlargement of vision, as I sensed within me, God saying these reassuring words - *'You can go to the ends of the earth, and I will still be with you; and between Tahiti and the UK, the whole world, Bob, is your parish'.* He had sent me to the ends of the earth to get a new perspective, and fresh direction. It wasn't necessarily that we would be travelling all over the place, but more that we would be relating with people from all the nations of the world. This was a big lesson for us in not putting limits on where God might send us! Frankly, God wants all of us to be available; to be willing to be sent anywhere that He may want to send us.

## PAUL'S SENSE OF TERRITORY

Paul had a general mandate to preach the gospel to the gentiles ('the nations'). He saw himself as *an apostle'* to them, rather than to his own people, the Jews (Gal.2:7-8). However, God had assigned to Paul specific geographical areas of activity, within which he would work at different stages in his ministry. To the Corinthians, Paul wrote, *'We will... confine our boasting to the field God has assigned us, a field that reaches even to you'* (2 Cor.10:13). He expressed his hope to them *'that...our area of activity among you will greatly expand, so that we can preach the gospel in the regions beyond you'* (2 Cor.10:15-16).

Paul, had a sense of calling to specific territories, and in the same way we can have a call to work in specific areas or regions.

## THE WORK DONE BY OTHERS

Paul's ambition was *'to preach the gospel where Christ was not known, so that I would not be building on someone else's foundation'* (Rom.15:20). He didn't *'want to boast about work done in another man's territory'* (2 Cor.10:16). He knew that God had assigned specific tasks for him to do, which were different to the assignments God had given to others. Paul never went to China or India, for example; it was the work of other apostles to go there.

It wasn't the case that Paul would not work with others. He was happy to recognise the tasks others were undertaking, even when they were situated in the same geographical area as himself. So, for example, regarding the church at Corinth, he wrote, *'What after all, is Apollos? And what is Paul? Only servants, through whom you came to believe - as the Lord has assigned to each his task. I planted the seed, Apollos watered it, but God made it grow'* (1 Cor.3:5-6).

Paul also knew that once he'd done his part, his work was over. He summed up his position in a letter to the Romans, that *'now there is no more place for me to work in these regions...'* (Rom.15:23). He was moving on to Spain, because he had completed all the assignments that God had given him in the other place (Rom.15:24).

## NEW TERRITORY IN THE NORTH

It can be difficult to move on, especially when you can see that there is still a lot of work that could be done in a particular area. For a number of years, Bob and I were working across London, and especially in four boroughs on the eastern side – an enormous field in which millions of people live, and where we could have worked for the rest of our lives!

However, God had chosen to stretch us, to increasingly work nationally (and internationally), while, at the same time, moving our regional base out of London to the north-east of England. This shift took a couple of years to make, and there were certain things we knew we had to complete, in order to leave – we were in the middle of a film-making project, for example, which required us to still live in London. Meanwhile, Bob was having an increasing ache to 'go home' (he comes from the North).

At first, he had thought God was being kind, and was accommodating him in his personal desire to move. It became increasingly clear, however, that God was in this shift of direction northwards! One day, when I was determined to get confirmation that we were on the right path, I prayed, asking God to give me a really clear word, if He wanted us to move north, as I was quite happy staying where I was! The very same day, I looked at a daily devotional, which I receive into my email box, the title was, "Heavenly alignment" and in it was God's word to me:- that, at this time 'God was moving His people into position for what was yet to come'; that 'He was in the move'; I was 'not to fear the uncomfortable shift', and that I was to 'set my compass to true North'! It could not have been clearer!

## A BIGGER SHIFT THAN EXPECTED

However, just when we were getting used to the idea of the shift north, we received several prophetic words which really changed the dynamic. They were about 'Norway', 'Oslo', and the Nordic countries generally. We had thought it was only about a move to the north of England, but God was also expanding our horizon, to encompass a much bigger idea of what the North might mean! So, even though we have put down our roots regionally, and made our local area the major arena for our work, we have also spent some time on ministry trips in the far north of Europe as well.

## THE GOD WHO OPENS DOORS

God opens doors to new territories, and shuts the doors on others. To the church at Philadelphia, Jesus calls himself the one *'who holds the key of David. What he opens no-one can shut, and what he shuts no-one can open...I have placed before you an open door that no-one can shut...'* (Rev.3:7-8). This is very reassuring! If a door needs opening for us to walk through, we can trust that God will open it, and make it clear when we are to walk through it. This was the promise God gave to Cyrus, that he would *'open doors before him'* (Isa.45:1). All of us can be reassured that our God will lead us into the things He has for us to do. *'For we are God's workmanship, created in Christ Jesus to do good works, which God prepared in advance for us to do'* (Eph.2:10).

## GOVERNORSHIP

In the time of Isaiah, there was a character called Eliakim, whom God had raised up as the governor over the King's palace in Judah. His name literally means, 'raised up by God'. In a prophetic pronouncement by Isaiah, he is symbolically given the key to the house of David, with the authority to open or shut any door in the palace. As the king's representative, he could do whatever he wanted, within the area assigned to him (Isa.22:15-25).

We had an experience of this in a strange way when we were university chaplains for a season in our lives. During this time, as chaplains, we experienced a freedom to move around the whole campus, and relate with both staff and students at every level. No-one quite knew what the job description of a chaplain entailed, and so we were allowed to write our own! Within the campus, we, and the other chaplains, carried an authority no-one could quite put their finger on! We were governors looking after all matters pertaining to the spiritual welfare of our domain, able to do whatever we felt God wanted us to do!

## PAUL'S GOVERNORSHIP

Paul wrote to the Colossians (Col.1:25) that, as a servant of the church, he had been given a *'governorship'* to present to them the word of God in its fullness. (The word 'governorship' is translated, *'commission'* in some versions.)

The Lord had opened up a door of understanding to him, concerning the mystery of what God had done in Christ, which he was now to proclaim. He described his preaching of the gospel to the Corinthians using the same word - as a *'governorship'* entrusted to him (1 Cor.9:17). Similarly, he wrote to the Ephesians, that he was *'looking after'* the mysteries that God had revealed to him for their sakes (Eph.3:2). Paul is using in all these references, the Greek word, *'oikonomia'* which primarily refers to the governance of a household. As a servant of the household of God, he was moving about his assigned territory.

God was opening and closing the doors to enable Paul to fulfil his governorship. So, for example, he wrote regarding Ephesus, *'...a great door for effective work has opened to me...'* (1 Cor.16:9). His prayer request to the Colossians was *'that God may open a door for our message, so that we may proclaim the mystery of Christ...'* (Col.4:3).

If God has assigned the territory, then He is the one who will open the doors for each one of us, so that we might be good governors, looking after our territory in all its daily detail. God has given us the keys to help us. Let's pray using the promise that Jesus gave to us, *'Ask and it will be given to you; seek and you will find; knock and the door will be opened to you'* (Mt.7:7).

## GOVERNING THE TERRITORY WITH WORSHIP

One key which expresses our governorship of the territory assigned to us, and declares God's rule, is our worship of the Lord.

As believers, when we first arrive in a place, we should understand that God has positioned us there, to be an altar of worship. Each of us presents our bodies as a living sacrifice to God, and He accepts it as our fitting worship to Him (Rom.12:1). As we hold Him up high in worship in our territories, His purposes are forwarded, and the enemy is silenced. Psalm eight tells us, *'From the lips of children and infants, you have ordained praise because of your enemies to silence the foe and the avenger'* (Ps.8:2). As an altar, we become a place of declaration that Jesus is Lord of this territory, and that we will serve him.

## PROPHETIC SINGING

When Mary and I were living in one London Borough, we heard God tell us to identify some of the physical locations there, which were of particular spiritual significance. We then felt led to bring together several worship teams, from across the area, to go to the different spots and 'flash mob' sing at them, on the same day, all at the same time. God was saying to 'sing from the mountaintops' in a prophetic, releasing way; to proclaim that His Kingdom had come! On the particular day that we had chosen, off we went, over eighty of us, to eight different locations, to sing out God's songs of blessing over the whole borough. We felt that we were being invited to join in with His mandate for the area, *'to preach the gospel to the poor, to heal the broken-hearted, to proclaim liberty to the captives and recovery of sight to the blind, to set at liberty those who are oppressed, to proclaim the acceptable year of the Lord'* (Lk.4:18-19). We were encouraged that our prophetic declarations were like keys, opening up doors in our territory.

## PRAYER WALKING THE TERRITORY

In one particular year, during our time in London, we also prayer-walked around the boundaries of a different London borough, over the course of three, separate days. This time, we felt that we were encouraging the believers there, to take spiritual responsibility for their patch along the boundary; a bit like the strategy that Nehemiah employed, in getting the families living in Jerusalem, to repair the wall adjacent to where they lived (Neh.3).

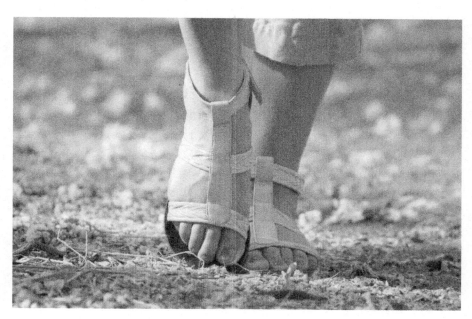

We also took part in 'Walk the Walls', a week-long prayer walk around London; one of several, which took place annually, at that time. As we walked, we had a real sense of possessing the territory and establishing God's Kingdom. The promise that God made to Joshua, we applied to ourselves –
*'I will give you every place where you set your foot'* (Josh.1:3).

When we prayer walk, we also listen to what God has to say about our area. As we open our ears to listen, He shows us things to pray for, so that doors might be opened, and our communities blessed and transformed by His love and power.

Worship, prayer and prophetic declarations help establish and maintain God's rule over the territories in which He has placed us.

You can read more about the prophetic singing and the prayer walking we did in our two books, 'Singing over Havering', and 'Prayer Walking around Redbridge' (available from Lulu and Amazon).

# PART TWO
# PARENTING

How apostles help us to grow up and mature as 'parents' ourselves, with Father's love for those around us.

# Thank you, Dad!

## A Bain family outing!
(from the archives!)

# Thank you, Dad!

Thank you for seeing the impossible
And reaching out for it;
For stretching and believing
For more than you can see
Around you now!

Thank you for inspiring me,
With a vision
That we can go somewhere
Together.

Thank you for delving into God's word
Digging for treasure,
Reaching for more
Further up and further in!
I love the excitement of life
With you.

Thank you for being a loving husband and father,
Encouraging, comforting,
Listening and believing
In me, in us;
In each of our children.

The sparkle and spontaneity;
I am enjoying the adventure,
As our boat bobs onwards,
With the sun shining down on us
And the peace of His presence
Holding us safe, always.

Mary Bain June 2016

# CHAPTER SEVEN
## THE PARENTING OF GOD

*God is in the parenting business. This is the great enterprise that apostles, and all of us, are engaged in, and we need to understand what it might look like.*

*God our Father - A parenting passage - The parenting aim - God's gifts have purpose - To be like Jesus - Becoming an adult -Fruitful discipline – Reproduction - Making disciples - 'In the name' - The Ascension gifts - Hidden labels - Recognition after death - 'One size fits all pastors' - No lost generation - Missing labels - A faithful father - Equipped for the work of service - Our early experiences of apostles*

## GOD OUR FATHER

The clue is in the name! Jesus, again and again, in the gospels refers to God as his Father, and taught his first disciples to pray, addressing God as *'Our Father in Heaven'*. Father God is in the parenting business. He has children. John the apostle tells us that those who have received Jesus, and believed in his name, are children of God, *'born not of natural descent, nor of human decision or a husband's will, but born of God'* (Jn.1:12-13).

## A PARENTING PASSAGE

There is a passage, written by Paul the apostle, in his letter to the Ephesian church, which is all about God as our Father, and how He parents His sons and daughters. (Eph.3:14 to 4:16).

It starts with Paul the apostle kneeling in prayer before Father God, *'from whom his whole family in heaven and on earth derives its name'*, and finishes with a vision of God's people grown up, equipped and mature.

In between, a process is described, which is, in its essence, a parenting one. Father God is raising His children to be adults. They are born, by the Holy Spirit, into God's family, but He isn't leaving them as spiritual babies.

## THE PARENTING AIM

From this passage in Ephesians, the aim of our Father God is that *'the body of Christ may be built up... and become mature, attaining to the whole measure of the fulness of Christ'* (Eph.4:12). Paul emphasises that God wants all of us to become mature; He isn't leaving any believers out! God is intimately engaged as a parent, with each one of us, *'until we all...become mature'* (Eph.4:12).

## TO BE LIKE JESUS

God's aim is that we might be like Jesus. He wants every child of God to be transformed into the likeness of His Son (2 Cor.3:18). John the apostle says, *'Now we are children of God, and what we will be has not yet been made known. But we know that when He appears, we shall be like him...'* (1 Jn.3:2).

## BECOMING AN ADULT

Parents raise their children with an eye on their destination. They know that one day their children will become adults. However cute babies may be we don't want them to stay forever in nappies! There is a time for babies to move on to the next stage. In fact, parents cannot stall what is happening at all – the growing process goes on regardless! Their desire is that their children will not just grow up, but will also become mature and responsible. In the same way, God wants His children to become spiritually mature and responsible.

Paul shared God's heart in his first letter to the Thessalonians. He tenderly described, in fatherly and motherly terms, how he had acted towards the church there. *'We were gentle among you, like a mother caring for her little children'* (1 Thess.2:7).

Again, he wrote, *'For you know that we dealt with each of you as a father deals with his own children, encouraging, comforting and urging you to live lives worthy of God'* (1 Thess.2:11-12). Paul is showing us the nature of God's parenting process, as he describes his own relationship, as an apostle, with the church. He likens it to the gentle encouragement and tenderness of a mother or father with their own children.

## FRUITFUL DISCIPLINE

However, the parenting process also involves discipline. *'God disciplines us for our good that we may share in His holiness'* (Heb.12:10). From a child's point of view, discipline may seem hard at times, and human parents can get it terribly wrong. However, let's not be put off by our experiences of bad parenting; God's parenting is different, and can be trusted.

God's fatherly discipline *'produces a harvest of righteousness and peace for those who have been trained by it'* (Heb.12:11). These are very reassuring words! There is something solidly fruitful and reproducible coming out from God's parenting. The fruit of the Spirit is being grown, which is *'love, joy, peace, patience, kindness, goodness, faithfulness, gentleness and self-control'* (Gal.5:22-23). Who wouldn't want these qualities of God's nature in their lives?

## REPRODUCTION

The English word, *'adult'* belongs to a family of words which all describe something being added to something else. So the root definition of, *'adult'* is to do with *'reproduction'*. Adults, male and female, each bring a reproductive component, which together creates a baby. (Negatively, in the same family of words, we have *adulterate*, where a pure substance is invaded by another substance, and *adultery*, where a marriage is invaded by an outsider to that marriage.)

So, children are raised by parents to become adults, i.e. potential parents themselves; equipped for reproduction. Sadly, not all adults who would like to have children are able to do so, and our understanding of what it means to be a fully grown person is a much broader one than the mere biological definition. However, in God's parenting of His children, all believers have the potential to spiritually reproduce.

## DISCIPLES MAKING DISCIPLES

We see this idea of reproducibility in the 'Great Commission' passage at the end of Matthew's gospel. Jesus commissions the disciples to *'go and make disciples of all nations, baptising them in the name of the Father, and of the Son, and of the Holy Spirit, and teaching them to obey everything I have commanded you'* (Mt.28:19-20). The first group of disciples was told by Jesus to make more disciples; everything they had been taught, they were now to pass on to others.

## 'IN THE NAME'

The disciples were told to baptise, that is, to immerse believers, into the <u>name</u> (the very nature and character) of God Himself.

When we say someone has a good name, or a bad name, we are using the word, <u>name</u>, in a similar way; to mean someone's nature - their character and identity, rather than simply what we call someone (e.g. whether they are a Tom, Dick or Harry!). The disciples, who were being baptised by the first disciples, would themselves become disciples, who, in turn, would go and make more disciples!

Unlike with natural parents, multiplication doesn't produce grandchildren and great grandchildren. All of these disciples become children of God with the same spiritual DNA. The same Holy Spirit has hovered over each in turn, and brought about a wonderful conception, and they have all become children of God, carrying the name of God, and growing in His nature and character.

## GOD'S GIFTS HAVE PURPOSE

The gifts that God has poured out graciously on His children have a parenting purpose. The Holy Spirit, the very breath of God, is within every believer in order to help in this purpose. Jesus described Him as *'the Helper'* (Jn.14:16). Since He is the Helper, so the gifts of the Spirit are there to help us – they are given to each one as the Spirit determines, and *'for the common good'* (1 Cor.12:7, 11). They are not there as an optional bonus for us to take or to leave. There is a purpose for them. Our Heavenly Father knows that His children have need of them, even as good human parents know what will be of benefit to their children.   Remember, the gifts of God are working towards an end result, namely that *'we will in all things grow up into him who is the Head, that is, Christ'* (Eph.4:15).

## THE ASCENSION GIFTS

The five Ascension gifts, which are helping us in God's parenting process, take the form of people! It is people who *'prepare God's people for the work of service'*. The Christian walk is not an isolated quest for enlightened maturity – God has given us people to help us.

*It was he [the Christ] who gave some to be apostles, some to be prophets, some to be evangelists, and some to be pastors and teachers...* (Eph.4:11).

Apostles, together with the other Ascension gifts, are an essential component in how God is maturing His church; a process which still continues today.

## HIDDEN LABELS

Throughout history, God has been using the five Ascension gifts. Generation after generation, they have been at work, even if they haven't always been recognized; and their work has sometimes continued under hidden labels. In some denominational circles today, for example, the term 'mission enabler' is used to describe a role that looks very much like that of an apostle!

## RECOGNITION AFTER DEATH

Sometimes, only after they have died, have apostles been recognised, and given their proper place within the work of God. For example, John MacDonald (1779-1849) was a Scottish minister who came to be known later as the 'Apostle of the North'. He wasn't the first. Anskar (801-865) was given the same title, by his successor, for his work in Northern Europe, but only after his death.

The official church of the day hadn't recognised either of them during their lifetimes.

## 'ONE-SIZE-FITS-ALL PASTORS'

Apostles, sensing a call on their lives but not understanding how to express it, can find themselves confused. They may not even realise that they are apostles. They have sometimes been lumped together, inappropriately, in the one-size-fits-all category of 'pastor', and squashed into doing pastoral things, alongside their real callings. In some of the streams, in which I flow, all church leaders are called 'Pastor', regardless of what their gifting and place in God's parenting process might actually be. How confusing is that!

## NO LOST GENERATION

There is good news however! God has been a patient Father with His church. There is no lost generation of His children. Every generation has felt His guiding hand on their lives.

All five gifts - apostle, prophet, evangelist, pastor and teacher – have functioned somehow, some way. In the muddle and confusion of things, they may not have been called those names, but they were still there, helping the church to grow to maturity! We can be confident that the Father has known how to bring up His children in every generation. He invented parenting, and He has always known what He was doing.

## MISSING LABELS

God loves us too much to leave us victims of the vagaries of church traditions. However, we could have saved ourselves a

lot of needless pain if we had got the labels right in the first place.

It reminds me of a story my father told. When he was a teenager, he went camping with some friends. They didn't have any paper to start the camp fire, so they had this great idea - they would use the labels from the food tins. Needless to say, they spent the rest of the holiday having some interesting combinations of food at meal times, as no one had a clue what was in the tins until they opened them! However, all the food they had brought with them was eaten in the end, even if the order of the menu was a bit crazy!

Similarly, the church has been fed and grown even when we have given apostles the wrong label, or no label at all!

## A FAITHFUL FATHER

*'Though my father and mother forsake me, the LORD will receive me'* (Ps.27:10).
Since the time of the early church, God has been a good parent to His children. Not one child has missed out. One way or another, we have all grown up. The *'one God and Father of all, who is over all, and through all, and in all'* (Eph.4:6) has been present in the whole process. No generation has ever been neglected and outsourced to others. It is not God's character to do this. He has been a faithful father.

Clearly, there is something which these five Ascension gifts bring to the table that is essential, for the growing-up process of God's sons and daughters. The absence of apostles, for example, from these five gifts, would have disabled the whole thing. Therefore, God has ensured their presence. There is no reason to think that there has ever been a change of plan.

# EQUIPPED FOR THE WORK OF SERVICE

Together, the Ascension gifts bring about a wonderful maturing of the body of Christ, as God graciously gives through them, all we need, for our particular *'work of service'* (Eph.4:12-13). They can be actively engaged in our lives, or just in the background like a catalyst, influencing the atmosphere. The chemistry truly works, and has been tried and tested over centuries.

With regards to apostles, Mary and I have had many experiences in which we have been helped by them. We didn't always realise that they were apostles at the time, and they probably didn't either, but nevertheless, they still gave us valuable input, at important moments in our lives.

## OUR EARLY EXPERIENCES OF APOSTLES

The first 'apostle' we encountered was at the start of our Christian life – he was a fellow student, on my Physics course at university. Mary and I had become Christians through the witness of a student group, to whom we are very grateful. However, we had all sorts of issues fitting in with this particular group. This was largely due to my questioning attitude, which they found hard to accommodate in their regular Bible studies.

Fortunately, our 'apostle' friend saw the problem, and created a group where my questions could be looked at. I found his personality very forceful and annoying at times, because he was deeply logical, and wouldn't let me fob off his arguments with shallow responses. Despite this, he did challenge me to examine how I'd arrived at the values and mindsets which I was holding, and made me realise that I was largely just repeating the popular world views of the time, without any thought of my own. At the same time, he opened up my mind to the amazing way in which the prophets in the Bible foreshadowed the coming of Jesus, his death and resurrection. This gave me confidence to look for God speaking to me, through the pages of the Bible.

So why do I think, my friend was an apostle, and not, for example, a teacher? Firstly, alongside his excellent teaching, he displayed leadership skills in establishing a group, when he saw that it was needed. Another indication was his understanding of the leadership potential in Mary and I, and how he encouraged us in it. He would let different ones lead the group, and prepare the talks. There would also be lots of discussion and personal application, to challenge us.

Some years later, we joined a newly formed church, which had started after some evangelistic healing meetings. It was being led by another 'apostle', who had stepped up to the challenge to establish this church. He created frameworks to encourage the church to grow, and gave opportunities for us to preach and lead meetings. He helped us to step out in a major decision to go to Bible College, and released us, with a prayer of blessing. We felt his support and encouragement throughout our training course, and later, following our graduation, he prayed a prayer of dedication over us, as we were installed as leaders in a local church elsewhere. He and his wife went on to work in Pakistan establishing churches, and creating leadership training programmes.

We salute and honour these two apostles, and are thankful to God for their timely input into our lives, which really helped to equip us in our calling. You may have your own outstanding examples of apostles to be thankful for, and may want to pause and consider how different ones have equipped you, for your work of service in God's family.

# CHAPTER EIGHT
## THE FIVE-FOLD GIFTED PARENT

*Comparisons can be made between the Ascension gifts and good parents. Since they are part of God's parenting process, apostles should be amazing father figures, but we don't want to fall into the trap of thinking they are the only ones. We are going to look at how apostles fit in alongside the other four gifts, by looking at how parents raise their children.*

*Parents reflect God's image*
*Parents as teachers*
>  *Practical instruction - Awesome wonder - Expressing emotions - The word in every season*
*Parents as pastors*
>  *Intimacy – Protection - Feed my lambs – Correction –*
>  *A Framework of Discipline*
*Parents as evangelists*
>  *Town-crier moments - Daily engagement - Signs and wonders*
*Parents as prophets*  .
>  *Recognising God's words - Words to treasure - Prophetic names - Prophetic songs - Bookmarks*
*Parents as apostles*
>  *Purpose and calling - The adventure of discovery – Establishing - Overview*
*God wants us all to be 'parents' - A growing self awareness – God is able*

## PARENTS REFLECT GOD'S IMAGE

Since God uses the Ascension gifts to mature His church, we would expect parents to also flow in these gifts, in the way in which they bring up their children. Parents are made in God's image, and so will reflect, in many ways, His type of parenting when raising their families. In a wonderful way,

God's own parenting heart is imaged in all who are engaged in parenting.

Jesus pulls on the comparison between human parents and our Heavenly Father, in Matthew's gospel. *'If you then, though you are evil, know how to give good gifts to your children, how much more will your Father in Heaven give good gifts to those who ask Him.'* (Mt.7:11). In a parallel passage in Luke, chapter eleven, it says that God our Father gives *'the Holy Spirit to those who ask Him'* (Lk.11:13).

When we look at how human parents raise their children, we can better understand what our Heavenly Father is doing through the Ascension gifts, in the church. Amazingly, parents provide a great model from which we can learn about the Ascension gifts. Parents understand instinctively that the gifting of apostles, prophets, evangelists, pastors and teachers, are an essential part of how they parent their children, even if they don't label what they are doing in those terms. We are going to look at all five gifts in the context of human parents, so we can particularly understand how apostles fit in, and function, within the parenting plan of God. This will hopefully prevent us from distorting the role of apostles, or, placing on them, exclusively, characteristics that are actually to do with the other four.

# PARENTS AS TEACHERS

So let's unpack the Ascension gifts from the parenting point of view starting in reverse order.

The teaching gift is an important function to have in any parent's toolkit.

# PRACTICAL INSTRUCTION

A good parent will want to instruct their children in every good thing, for their building up and ongoing blessing.

<u>Proverbs</u> is a great book to refer to, for practical instruction about life – *'My son do not forget my teaching but keep my commands in your heart, for they will prolong your life many years and bring you prosperity'* (Prov.3:1-2). There is a practical edge to a parent's teaching; wisdom to convey, that has been forged in the experiences of life, and is now being passed on to the child, to be applied and proved true in his own life.

One lesson, for example, encouraging children to work hard, is found in Proverbs chapter 6, *'Go to the ant, you sluggard; consider its ways and be wise…A little sleep, a little slumber, a little folding of the hands to rest – and poverty will come on you like a bandit, scarcity like an armed man'*

# AWESOME WONDER

There is also a wonder to be conveyed, and a proper understanding of our place in creation. Examples of this are seen in the book of Job.

In the closing chapters of the book (chapters 38 to 41), God speaks to Job in order to bring some wonder and awe into his thinking. For example, in Job 38:31-32, the Lord invites him to look at the stars in the night sky, and says, *'Can you bind the beautiful Pleiades? Can you loose the cords of Orion? Can you bring forth the constellations in their seasons or lead out the Bear with its cubs? Do you know the laws of the heavens? Can you set up God's dominion over the earth?* '

In Job chapter thirty-nine the wonder of the natural world is laid before us in many examples of different birds and animals. For example, *'Does the hawk take flight by your wisdom and spread his wings towards the south? Does the eagle soar at your command and build his nest on high?'* (Job 38:26-27).

The Psalms bring to us all the wonder of worship. Good parents will want to spend time worshipping with their children, and also model to them their thankfulness to God, *'Let the word of Christ dwell in you richly as you teach and admonish one another with all wisdom and as you sing psalms, hymns and songs in the spirit with gratitude in your hearts to God'* (Col.3:16).

## EXPRESSING EMOTIONS

The Psalms also show us how we can express our emotions to the Lord, when things are not working out like we think they should. *'Why are you downcast, O my soul? Why so disturbed within me? Put your hope in God, for I will yet praise Him, my Saviour and my God'* (Ps.42:5).

Good parents teach their children to pray with reality and fullness of feeling, to the Lord. Children need to learn that the difficulties in life they may be experiencing have their resolution in a prayerful relationship with God.

## THE WORD IN EVERY SEASON

A good parent will also want to teach the importance of the word of God, in every season of life.

Psalm 119 is like a teaching song about God's word. It goes through the whole Hebrew alphabet in twenty-two sections to tell us that the word of God matters in every stage of life, from the start of the alphabet to the end. By the time you have sung your way through the whole psalm, you are left in no doubt that you should listen up to what God has to say to you! Parents also encourage their children through reading Bible stories with them, and talking about them, as well as modelling their own dependence and daily trust in God's words.

# PARENTS AS PASTORS

Parents are pastors to their family. A pastor is really just another word for shepherd. So how is the parenting process of Father God being modelled by parents, when they function as pastors? Jesus described himself as the good shepherd in John, chapter ten, so let's go there, to understand more about how parents are pastors to their children.

## INTIMACY

Parents intimately know their children, like good shepherds know their sheep. Jesus says in John, chapter ten, *'I am the good shepherd. I know my sheep and my sheep know me – just as the Father knows me, and I know the Father...'* (Jn.10:14-15).

Parents and children are constantly in one another's lives. They know one another's moods, and even, every tone of voice. Parents have been there in every high and low; in every rough and tumble of their children's lives. They usually understand their children more intimately than anyone else.

## PROTECTION

Just as Jesus the good shepherd lays down his life for the sheep (Jn.10:11), supremely, good parents will lay down their lives for their children. They do their best to protect them from every danger, just as the shepherd protects his sheep from predators.

The heart of Jesus is expressed tenderly, in Matthew's gospel, as that of a distressed mother hen longing to protect her children. *'O Jerusalem…how often I have longed to gather your children together as a hen gathers her chicks under her wings, but you were not willing'* (Mt.23:37). Paul also identifies himself with the same mother's heart, when he says, *'We were gentle among you, like a mother caring for her little children. We loved you so much that we were delighted to share with you not only the gospel of God but our lives as well because you had become so dear to us'* (1 Thess.2:7-8). This is Paul sacrificially sharing of himself, even up to the point of death itself! Parents have this same pastor's heart, seen in their instinctive desire to protect their children from harm.

## FEED MY LAMBS

A major aspect of parenting is one involving the food cupboard! After his resurrection, Jesus appears to Peter by the shores of Galilee. He gives Peter his final instructions. *'Feed my lambs'*, *'Take care of my sheep'* and *'Feed my sheep'* (Jn.21:15-17). The over-riding concern of Jesus is that Peter feeds and cares for the flock.

Good parents do their best to nourish and nurture their children, not only by feeding their bodies, but also their minds, emotions and spirits as well.

## CORRECTION

*'All scripture is God-breathed and is useful for teaching, rebuking, correcting and training in righteousness, so that the man of God may be thoroughly equipped for every good work'* (2 Tim.3:16-17). Parents, in their pastoral care of their children, will need, from time to time, to rebuke them, correcting their behaviour and helping to train them in the right direction. They also want their children to learn how to discipline themselves, and to stay on the track that leads to life and peace, and not trouble or destruction.

## A FRAMEWORK OF DISCIPLINE

In my late teens, I had a vacation job, working in the glasshouses near our home. They grew a lot of cucumbers, and I really enjoyed working there in the summer months, going up and down the shady rows. It was especially nice when the rain was pounding down on the glass frames, because inside, it was all very tropical and cosy.

However, the cucumber plants weren't always easy to look after. When I worked in the glasshouses in the Easter holiday, the young cucumber plants were still sprouting up and spreading outwards along the earth. Our job was to go along the rows, gently lifting them up and curling them around strings, hanging down vertically, for that purpose. The framework of string was there ready for them, but the cucumber plants needed to be set off in the right direction if they were to produce a good crop. They had to be pointed upwards, away from the dirt and grubbiness of the ground.

We can see from these illustrations that discipline is not so much about punishment, but about guiding children clearly and firmly in the way that will bring blessing and fruitfulness to them. Parents put a framework up, and then encourage their children to grow up around it. However, parents as pastors will have to exert discipline, on the occasions when the child does stray away from the framework. This will be an unpleasant but memorable experience for the child, and hopefully one from which they will learn!

# PARENTS AS EVANGELISTS

So how is the parenting process of Father God being modelled by parents, when they function as evangelists? Every Christian parent wants to make sure their child knows about the gospel – the good news that there is a way to live an abundant life in God, and to be with Him forever. Parents understand that their children won't automatically become children of light, born of God and in the family of God. Just as their parents did, they must decide, themselves, to come to God through Jesus. Children need to have the good news shared with them. Parents have a life-time assignment from God to be His ambassadors to their own children.

# TOWN-CRIER MOMENTS

Like a good, old-fashioned town crier, parents may feel inclined to just unroll their scroll, and shout out, *'Salvation is found in no-one else but Jesus, for there is no other name under heaven given to men by which we must be saved'* (Acts 4:12).

It may be that there will be occasions when they should do that! Joshua had that kind of a moment, when he cried out to the people of Israel, *'Now fear the Lord… choose for yourselves this day whom you will serve… as for me and my household we will serve the Lord'* (Josh.24:14-15). Some days arrive with that kind of gravity about them – important days of decision. It is a wonderful moment to hear one's children say that they have received Jesus into their lives. No longer is God an external truth that they have gone along with, as part of their family's cultural heritage, but He has become their personal Saviour. Sometimes this can happen all at once, but usually there has been a process of learning about Jesus over several years.

# DAILY ENGAGEMENT

Parents evangelise their children through the daily engagements of their lives. Every interaction with their children has the opportunity of being evangelistic.

Jesus called his first disciples to be 'fishers of men'. Some of them had actually been fishermen, and the skills and patience of that work, were now being transferred into the work of evangelism. Parents need that same skill and patience to persevere in conveying the good news of the gospel to their children.

Parents spread nets, at the times and places, when and where they know that the fish/children are likely to be around! The good news has to be made accessible and attractive, however! So parents will take time to connect with their children, and also pray that they will be there at the right moments to help them to come to Jesus. In the teenage years, some fish don't emerge well in the mornings, but by midnight they are up for a conversation! Younger ones will be scampering about in the early hours of dawn, so a walk in the park with them, at that time, may be a wonderful moment to convey the love of God.

Story times before bed give opportunities to tell the stories and experiences of others, as well as the story of God's love for all mankind in sending Jesus. The seasons of the year, and the cultural events in the calendar, can also act as evangelistic landmarks to point children towards God.

Words, not just spoken, but also demonstrated by parents, who uphold God's love and the truth of the gospel, will always make an impact on the lives of their children.

## SIGNS AND WONDERS

The book of Acts, chapter eight, records that the crowds in Samaria listened carefully to Philip the evangelist, as he proclaimed the gospel message along with miraculous signs. *'With shrieks, unclean spirits came out of many, and many paralytics and cripples were healed'* (Acts 8:6-7).

There have been times in our family life, when Mary and I have cried out to God for the needs of our children, and he has given us the boldness and faith to declare words of life over them, which have dramatically changed the situation. One such occasion happened when one of our sons had a cycling accident. He was being rushed into the operating theatre with a possibility that he may not come out alive! We both began to speak out promises from the Bible, and are thankful that today he is very much alive and healthy. The power of God was very evident to the whole family!

However, even in the ordinary matters of living, the provision of God can be so obvious, that it has been a sign to our children that God is indeed real, and not some kind of parental fantasy! What looked like disaster has been turned around. What looked like a brick wall dead-end, has suddenly has an open door in it! For example, the finances arrive just in time; there is food on the table when there was none the day before; the passport is found; the car starts; there is healing rather than long term complications and difficulties.

Signs and wonders are also an opportunity for parents to be evangelists to their children.

# PARENTS AS PROPHETS

So how is the parenting process of Father God being modeled by parents, when they function as prophets? *'Everyone who prophesies speaks to men for their strengthening, encouraging and comfort'* (1Cor.14:3). What parent wouldn't want to strengthen, encourage and comfort their children? The wonder of prophecy is that God can use parents to speak out His words, to do just that. They can find themselves speaking out just the right words for that moment, bringing encouragement and comfort from the Lord.

## RECOGNISING GOD'S WORDS

A Christian parent will also want to encourage their children to go on a journey of recognising God's voice for themselves. They can help to facilitate this; so that instead of feeling intimidated, their children will begin to step out in hearing and speaking out words from God, that will encourage and build up those around them, as well as themselves.

When the boy, Samuel, heard from God, he didn't at first recognise who was speaking, and thought that the priest, Eli, had been calling out for him. After this happened three times in a row, Eli, perhaps motivated by getting a good night's sleep, wisely pointed Samuel in the right direction, making it clear that it was God's voice speaking to him. Eli also helped Samuel to find the correct vocabulary to respond to God - next time say, *'Speak, for your servant is listening'* (1 Sam 3:10). Parents, when acting as prophets, should open up their children to the possibility that they can hear from God, and that, in spite of their age, God can use <u>them</u> to prophesy to others.

## WORDS TO TREASURE

Some prophetic words are for the parents to treasure up, and ponder about, just as Mary did. *'Mary treasured all these things in her heart'* (Lk.2:19, 49, 51).
God was clearly at work doing something amazing around the birth of Jesus. At the time, it was enough for Mary to allow the full significance of the prophetic words spoken to her, to unfold as her child grew up. But, later, when she heard her son's words in the Temple, *'Didn't you know I had to be in my Father's house?'* her eyes were opened even further to who Jesus really was.

Sometimes, like Mary, parents may hear big words for their children. They may also recognize that these words are not for immediate strengthening and encouragement, or warning dreams that require immediate action. They are actually words to treasure and hold onto for their child's future; speaking into the bigger picture of their child's identity and calling.

## PROPHETIC NAMES

There is a tremendous privilege placed upon parents at the birth of their children – the giving of their names. This really is an important prophetic moment. Mary and I prayed to God, that the names which we gave to each of our children would be a word from Him over their lives. We felt it was important that that their names carried a meaning with them. So, for example, our eldest son's name, David, means 'Beloved' or 'Friend'.

## PROPHETIC SONGS

When our children were little, I asked the Lord to give me a fun song for each of them. I prayed about the meaning of the names, which Mary and I had chosen, and also looked at some of the scriptures that had been spoken out at each of their dedications. I put the words together with some simple guitar chords and really enjoyed singing them out! I felt that each song carried a prophetic meaning, and was a kind of prayer for them. So, for example, our son, Joseph's name means, 'He adds blessing'; and I came up with the line, 'He's a wise little blessing who adds fun, fun, fun, fun!' Then, and now, as a grown-up married man, Joseph continues to do just that. He is indeed a wise blessing, who has brought much fun to those around him. I believe these songs, however light and trivial they might have sounded, were speaking out God's words over our children.

## BOOKMARKS

Much later, when our children were in their teens, or already adults, I had the idea of creating a special bookmark one Christmas, for each of them. We have seven children, and Mary and I spent many hours, getting prophetic pictures, scripture verses and some prayer words which we felt were important for them, at that time of their lives, and into the future.

It was certainly a helpful exercise as a parent, to ponder over what the Lord might be saying about our children, and it helped us to pray for them. I believe it has also blessed them, as they considered their own personal bookmark.

As parents, it is good to be open to hearing words for our children. We can also encourage them to hear for themselves what God might be speaking out over them, at different 'bookmark' moments in their lives.

# PARENTS AS APOSTLES

So how is the parenting process of Father God being modelled by parents when they function as apostles?
We have considered parenting in terms of the other four Ascension gifts – this should help us to have a clearer idea of the unique characteristics which the apostle brings.

## PURPOSE AND CALLING

Parents help establish a sense of purpose and calling in their children's lives. Every child needs to understand that he is born into the world with a unique, God-given calling and purpose. God has shaped and formed them, in terms of their personalities, temperaments, skills and abilities, in such a way that they can fulfill completely, His will for their lives. They have been sent out into the world with purpose. The job of parents is to convey this sense of 'sentness'.

In effect, parents are 'apostle-ing' their children, when they open up to them the bigger picture of themselves as being born with a purpose.

## THE ADVENTURE OF DISCOVERY

Parents take their children on an exciting adventure of discovery of the world around them, and their place in it.

Education is not the child's equivalent of the world of work, it is not even training in skills, nor the receiving of knowledge, but a person's process of discovery, and formation of themselves. The word, 'educate' comes from a Latin word that means, 'to lead out'. Parents are involved in the leading out of their children into maturity. They introduce them to new experiences, in which they find out more about themselves, and their identity.

## BUILDING AND ESTABLISHING

Parents are not only there to help their children understand their purpose in life, but also to help establish them in it. They should not impose their own dream list ideas of what they would like their child to become. They are there to work in partnership with God, with the materials as presented to them!

Good parents help to facilitate a building process; they encourage and support their children to keep going; to enjoy who they are, and to grow into the person whom God has called them to be.

## OVERVIEW

It is important for parents to give their children an overview, to help them stay true to God's plan. Their children may need some help to read the road map, which will get each one to where they need to be. Parents can also help by being on the look-out to connect their children with opportunities, which are in line with God's plan.

From time to time, their children's attitudes may need challenging and disturbing, so that they continue to move forward and any bad fruit forming in their lives, withers on the vine.

# CONCLUSION

## A GROWING SELF-AWARENESS

As children of God, we have a growing self-awareness of the parenting work of God in our lives. The longer we have known God, the more we have come to realise that we are on a trajectory; to be filled to the measure of all the fullness of God (Eph.3:19). All along the way, the power of God has been at work within us, acting for our benefit. Our Heavenly Father has been engaging with us in a comprehensive process, which has involved every part of our being.

As earthly children, we were just soaking up the love, and eating the weetabix, and engaging with those things that our parents were presenting to us; but as we matured, we realised the extent of the process that had been going on, and came to a place of thankfulness, and appreciation for our natural parents. It is the same for us, as children of God with our Heavenly Father; our growing awareness of His work in our lives, fills us with gratitude, and we give Him all the glory.

## GOD IS ABLE

How can this amazing maturing into parenthood come about? It is beyond us to figure it out! We must humbly come into position in the body of Jesus, and do those things which God is calling us to do. We can't take on someone else's life or calling. We can only live our own lives. It is enough to be who we are called to be, in the position into which God has placed us.

It all starts in the place of prayer, in humility and surrender to God our Father. This is where Paul started, at the beginning of the parenting passage, from Ephesians, *'I kneel before the Father from whom the whole family [from whom all fatherhood] in Heaven and on Earth derives its name [nature and being]'* (Eph 3:14-15).

Paul kneels, opens his mouth and prays, *'that out of His glorious riches, He may strengthen you with power through His Spirit in your inner being...'* (Eph.3:16-19).
It is no wonder that he concludes his prayer by saying that God is *'able to do immeasurably more than all we could ask or imagine...'* (Eph 3:20). However impossible it seems, God has been at work in us, changing and maturing us *'from one degree of glory to another'* (2Cor.4:16).

## GOD WANTS US ALL TO BE 'PARENTS'

God's desire for all of us is that we become 'parents' to those around us - in church life, our communities, schools and places of work. The world is desperately in need of fathers and mothers! By looking at all five of these Ascension gifts in turn, in the context of human parents, we have seen that they are all involved in the parenting of church and community. In the church, each Ascension gift can be a father or mother figure to us, to help us all to come to maturity. When they are doing their jobs well, these fathers or mothers act as 'parents,' raising us to the same level of maturity as themselves. This is the amazing enterprise that all of us, are engaged in!

# PART THREE
# BUILDING

How apostles help us to relate and build one another up in our normal, ordinary lives – connecting, communicating, encouraging and supporting, disturbing and disrupting, and working with others as a team.

# CHAPTER NINE
# HIDDEN AND UNPREDICTABLE

*There is a hidden quality about much of the building work of apostles. More is going on than we may realise at first, in the way in which they are helping us. This is a different kind of work to that with bricks and mortar.*

*Underground animals - Hidden in the ordinary - More under the surface - A bigger story - Leadership is influence - Mother and father figures – Teaching - Hidden foundations – Unpredictable – Led to Macedonia – Led to Philippi*

## UNDERGROUND ANIMALS

A few years ago, Mary and I had some reassuring words from the Lord. They were reassuring, because they helped us to understand what our own connecting and encouraging work, across the church, might look like. They gave us some insights into how we fitted in. I often describe them as 'popping up' words, because they all featured animals that live underground, but pop up to the surface at different times. There were three animals which the Lord gave us to consider - *rabbits, gophers and moles.* Yes, odd, isn't it? All I can say is the Bible does tell us to consider the ant (Prov.6:6) and the birds of the air (Mt.6:2), so why not rabbits, gophers and moles?

Over the course of a few months, sometimes in the context of prayer, but at other times in everyday conversations, one at a time, these three animals were highlighted to us. We sensed, on each occasion, that God was telling us to listen up and to learn something. Each animal word was a prophetic picture clarifying aspects of our work and how to go about it. The timing was brilliant as we were about to move to the North East of England, and we were asking God about the work that

He had for us to do there; as well as in other parts of the UK and beyond.

## HIDDEN IN THE ORDINARY

The work of an apostle doesn't have to be a highly visible one. I thought it was particularly apt that the words we had received were all about <u>underground</u> animals, who have the ability to be hidden from view. Much of the work of an apostle is like that! There may be spectacular, highly visible moments, but a lot is hidden in the ordinary. When Paul tells the church at Corinth to imitate his way of life, he wants them to follow the example of his ordinariness – how he handles his everyday life, from day to day. He sends Timothy to remind the church of his way of life in Christ Jesus - his regular routines and conduct towards others (1 Cor.4:16-17). Paul is not veiling his humanity in a magical fog of smoke and mirrors, maintaining a special status, by keeping aloof from everyone else. He wants them to see him as he really is.

Mary and I once met this wonderful couple, at a meeting. We were young Christians, in our twenties, at the time. The couple sat down and chatted to us, while we waited for the programme to begin. It was only at this point as they stepped up onto the platform that we realized they were the main speakers! They began the meeting by sharing some of the amazing things from their mission experiences around the world. The extraordinary thing was how normal they were! Their capacity to walk humbly and ordinarily through the most head-spinning circumstances was extraordinary. The glory was hidden in the ordinary. They were carrying their treasure in very ordinary jars of clay, and at the end of the day, they were content to say that they were only servants, who had done their duty. (Lk.17:10).

This is one important lesson about humility and grace which we can learn from our underground animals.

## MORE UNDER THE SURFACE

When we read Paul's letters, we get the feeling that there is more going on off-stage, in the hidden place of intimacy with God, than what can be seen onstage! What may be out of sight is having a profound effect on what we can actually see.

Paul is the proverbial iceberg, most of which is under the surface! He tells us that he knows a man, who has seen unspeakable mysteries, in heavenly places. Of course, we are meant to understand that this man is him! (2 Cor.12:2-4). As we read his letters, our eyes are opened to a deeper, hidden intimacy which he has been experiencing with God, behind the scenes. We get a glimpse into what Paul's prayer life was like, when he tells the Colossians, for example, that he is constantly praying for them (Col.1:9). He also says to the

Corinthian church how he prays in tongues more than all of them (1 Cor.14:18).

So another lesson which we can learn from our underground animals is to imitate their hidden life. There is a wonderful place into which God is calling us – to come under the shadow of His wings; an important, hidden place of homeliness and intimacy, deep under the surface with Him.

## A BIGGER STORY

The list of some of the hardships and dangers that Paul experienced during his life, is so quickly rattled off, in one letter, that we hardly have a chance to take in what he has said.

*'Five times I received from the Jews the forty lashes minus one. Three times I was beaten with rods, once I was stoned, three times I was shipwrecked, I spent a night and a day in the open sea. I have been constantly on the move. I have been in danger from rivers, in danger from bandits, in danger...in danger... I have often gone without sleep...often gone without food'* (2 Cor.11:24-27). When we read this, we begin to realise that we know hardly anything about what Paul had really gone through, away from the public eye. The Acts of the Apostles hardly scratches the surface of it!

Just like the underground animals, the fuller story of what is going on in our lives is unlikely to be known by others around us. Mary and I have been through all sorts of things; done all sorts of things (as all of us have). We have been sons and daughters, parents and grandparents. I have no desire to time-travel and experience again the pain and the joy of any of it, but the lessons learnt can certainly help us, in the present. They are a bigger story, hidden from sight, which we can ask God to redeem and use, as a blessing to help others. On the surface, they also add weight to what we are saying, because people sense that we have been round the block a few times, and could have something of value to share, which might help them to make wise choices in their own lives. It is a good attitude to have, whenever we meet people – to understand that everyone has a story, and that we can definitely learn something from listening to it!

## LEADERSHIP IS INFLUENCE

One famous quote from John Maxwell's books on developing leadership qualities says that 'leadership is influence'.

In the context of the church, many have reduced leadership to the arena of a local congregation, and judge a leader's success by the number of people attending the church. However, Paul was not interested in how many followers he had. He wasn't leading a local church, and certainly would have had difficulty defining his role in those terms. He told the Corinthian church that he thanked God that he had not gathered a following, who could say, *'I am of Paul'* (1 Cor.1:12). He wasn't parading himself at the front of a crowd, comparing his 'success' with others. However, <u>he did want to influence</u> them.

## MOTHER AND FATHER FIGURES

Something more organic and relational was going on in Paul's interactions with the Corinthian church. He had birthed them, and he saw them as his children (1 Cor.4:14, 2 Cor.6:13).

He writes, *'...In Christ Jesus I became your father through the gospel'* (1 Cor.4:15). The evidence of his leadership was founded on the history of his relationship with them as a father. In one letter to another church, Paul described how he was once again in the pangs of child birth, until Christ was formed in them (Gal.4:19). To a different church, he described himself both as a father and a mother in his behaviour towards them (1 Thess.2:7, 11).

Coming into a room, you might not, at first glance, recognise the hidden relationship connections between the people; for example you may not easily spot who is someone's mother or someone else's daughter, but, to be sure, the connections are there, influencing what is going on! All a casual observer might see are the people, but look closely, and you will see that under the clothes, they all have belly buttons! Everyone, in the physical sense has been birthed by someone, and grown up being influenced by parents or parental figures. Christians have mother and father figures, who have influenced them. They have been birthed through the gospel in different settings, and, hidden from sight, there have been significant people who have influenced and impacted their lives.

## TEACHING

Leadership by influence also has a teaching element to it. Of course, teaching and learning something, are not the same thing, but a good teacher will always inspire his students to learn. When Jesus warned his disciples to beware of the leaven of the Pharisees, he was referring to what they were teaching - their influence on people's lives, and he warned his disciples, not to learn from these teachers (Mt.16:11-12).

On a more positive note, Jesus goes on to teach that the Kingdom of God is like a woman making bread. She kneads the dough and eventually the leaven works through the whole lump (Mt.13:33). This is a hidden process but in the end the yeast is worked into the whole lump, and affects it all.

When teaching in the various churches, Paul would know if he had done his work well, because the result on the surface would finally become self-evident. There is a waiting time while the yeast, hidden from sight, is doing its work, and also the baker has to create the right conditions; but in the end, if all is done well, the dough will rise and make a good loaf!

In the case of Paul's teaching, the final loaf has been made available to people all through the ages! He has been an influence throughout my own Christian life, even as he has influenced millions before me! Through the Holy Spirit, Paul's teaching to Christians in those early churches, has also worked on my heart, and I have become a letter from Christ - the result of his ministry!

Paul was able to say to the Corinthian church at the time that he had been at work in their lives through his teaching, and, as a result, they had become a wonderful letter from Christ. They were a far more powerful commendation of his leadership than any written letter would have been (2 Cor.3:2).

## HIDDEN FOUNDATIONS

Paul tells us that the foundations of the church are the apostles and prophets, with Christ as the chief cornerstone (Eph.2:20). The foundation of a building is a hidden thing, yet the whole stability of the building depends on it. If a building stands straight and tall, unmoved by storms and trials, then it is built on good foundations. You don't get to see the foundations, but you do get to see the results, especially in adversity!

In another of his letters, Paul talks of apostles as the most despised and little-recognised group of all. They are at the end of the triumphal procession – an afterthought, considered hardly worth including in the parade. Their presence is barely noticed by the crowds, who have failed to recognise the key foundational role they have played. If apostles have done their job well, they will be easily overlooked (1 Cor.4:9); but just like the foundations of a building, apostles are actually undergirding and supporting everything that is going on.

# UNPREDICTABLE

Apostles also have the habit of showing up unexpectedly. One moment they are hidden, but the next moment they are popping up! There is an element of unpredictability in their actions and movements. Like the underground animals, which we felt the Lord had pointed out to Mary and I, apostles can possess a 'popping-up' unpredictability! Suddenly they arrive on the surface - they have 'popped up' in a church or a region; and their gifting, has a visible role to play.

This is a challenging characteristic for us to embrace as church, if we like our calendars to be orderly and routine. However, unpredictability comes with firm scriptural backing.
_The wind blows wherever it pleases._ _You hear its sound but you cannot tell where it comes from or where it is going. So it is with everyone born of the Spirit.'_ (Jn.3:8).

The Holy Spirit, like the wind, blows wherever He pleases. He is the one whom Jesus promised would come, to guide and direct every believer, and He is described in this passage as being like the wind blowing wherever He pleases. So we should expect His direction and guidance to be unpredictable.

The 'everyone' mentioned in this passage, is _'everyone born of the Spirit'_. So, all believers have to realise that they too have this unpredictable characteristic about them! They can also be like the wind, blown where the Spirit directs them. Therefore, every believer needs to be prepared for unexpected changes in direction. God has surprising appointments ahead, written in invisible ink in our diaries!

Paul says in Romans chapter eight, _'Those who are led by the Spirit of God are sons of God'_ (Rom.8:14). In Galatians, he says,

*'Walk by the Spirit'* (Gal.5:16). Walking, and being led by the Spirit, comes with surprises, because the Spirit who is leading us is like the wind – completely unpredictable. There is an element of surprise to expect in what any believer might do, when led by the Spirit. Unpredictability is a     predictable characteristic of the Holy Spirit! It is hardly surprising, then, that apostles should display this 'popping-up' unpredictability. Every believer should be open to it, and apostles, when they do behave unpredictably, are a helpful model for all of us!

## LED TO MACEDONIA

There is a good example of apostles being led unexpectedly in Acts, chapter sixteen. It records that Paul was on mission with Silas, Timothy and Luke in the region of Phrygia and Galatia. Clearly, they were engaged in a listening process and open to the direction of the Holy Spirit. A changing sequence of travel is described. *'They had been kept by the Holy Spirit from preaching the word in the province of Asia. When they came to the border of Mysia, they tried to enter Bithynia, but the Spirit of Jesus would not allow them to'* (Acts 16:6-7). This is language describing a group being led by the Spirit. After this, Paul suddenly has a vision, during the night, of a man from Macedonia, standing and begging him to come over to help them. Paul concludes that this is the leading of the Holy Spirit and immediately they set off for Macedonia! Traditional sources point to the apostle, Andrew, being at work, preaching the gospel, in the other direction; so there would have been no need for Paul to go there. The Holy Spirit knew this, even if Paul didn't, and so He made sure that Paul travelled on, to a different assignment, elsewhere.

## LED TO PHILIPPI

Another example of unpredictability occurs a few days later.

Paul and the others in his party arrive in Philippi, the leading city of Macedonia, and surface in the life of a lady called Lydia. Her regular routine was about to be disturbed through an encounter with an apostle! Lydia was in the habit of going down to the river to pray each Sabbath , but this time her whole life was about to be turned around, as Paul meets her along with the group of ladies praying there, and shares the gospel with them. Lydia believes in Jesus, and her whole life is set off in a new direction (Acts.16:13-15). An apostle had 'popped up' and changed everything!

# CHAPTER TEN
# COMMUNICATIONS
# AND CONNECTIONS

*Apostles spend a lot of time bringing people together and making connections. Communications are at the heart of their work; they are not an afterthought. The health of the church depends on them. They are essential in helping it grow.*

*Rabbits - - Communicating foundational experiences - Apostles as communicators – Letters - Maintaining connections - The human connection – Greetings – News - Reports and evidence - Communicating arrangements – Letters of Recommendation - Travel help - Our experience*

## RABBITS

We felt that it was so spot-on of the Lord to draw our attention to rabbits, in the words we were given. We sensed that God was saying something about connections and communications through them. Rabbits may do a lot of popping up above ground but, below the surface, they are involved in a lot of hidden connectivity. Beneath the ground the rabbit warren is a maze of connecting tunnels, which are supporting what we get to see on the surface. You don't see the warren but it's there.

## COMMUNICATING FOUNDATIONAL EXPERIENCES

Communication is a hidden work, but amazingly, also in plain sight! When we sit down with the New Testament, we are actually reading the communications of the early apostles. Whether we are reading the gospels, the letters or the visions in Revelation, we are being communicated with, through their written words. The gospels, for example, were written down as the first-hand accounts of those who had witnessed the public ministry, death and resurrection of Jesus. They are the foundational experiences of those who had actually been with Jesus, being communicated to us today!

When the eleven apostles were deciding who might replace Judas, in Acts chapter one, they chose someone who had been *with Jesus*. In Peter's words, *'It is necessary to choose one of the men who have been with us the whole time the Lord Jesus went in and out among us, beginning from John's baptism to the time when Jesus was taken up from us. For one of these must become a witness with us of His resurrection'* (Acts 1:21-22). It was out of their experiences of being with Jesus, of living their lives with him, that the gospels were written, either by the apostles, or by those associated with them. In this way, the Holy Spirit was ensuring that their witness to the public life of Jesus, from John's baptism to the resurrection of Jesus, would be communicated to everybody, from those early times right up to the present day.

Although not to be enshrined as scripture, there are foundational experiences which apostles, in any generation, need to communicate. These are key experiences with the Lord, which have shaped their lives, and sharing them, will be of benefit to others. The telling of these key experiences can show us, for example, how important it is for each of us to reflect on our own stories, and share them with those around us, as the Lord leads. Every grand-parent needs to know that, as they share the good and the bad experiences of their lives, they are passing on a legacy from which their grandchildren can learn.

These foundational experiences of our lives need to be communicated with the next generation, and apostles can encourage this. They are not the only ones with a story, and they can play a key role in facilitating others to tell their stories as well.

## APOSTLES AS COMMUNICATORS

This really is a basic statement - apostles are communicators! One part of their role is to ensure that good communications and connections are happening across the church. In New Testament times, this could be done by letter, or by a personal visit, or simply by sending someone on their behalf. Connections were being made across the whole church through a constant stream of communication, initiated by apostles.

## LETTERS

Letters were an important part of the communications in the early church. The letters that we read in the New Testament are a collection of real letters, all written by apostles. They were written for real recipients, for a particular moment. The early apostles wrote what they felt a church, or an individual, needed to read, to help them at that time, and in that situation.

When we look at the letters in the New Testament, we can see that the range of content is quite wide. All sorts of issues were being addressed; the letters were certainly not written as abstract essays! They are communications to real people, who needed to be connected with at that time, and in that way. The apostles knew that if they were to do their job properly, they would need to keep communicating in helpful ways with the churches. They sensed the urgency to write! Of course, as we read the letters, we get to be communicated with and encouraged as well! Letters written for a particular time and place have had the uncanny ability to be helpful to many others, over the centuries. How amazing is that!

## MAINTAINING CONNECTIONS

Once they have been made, connections need to be maintained. This is a never-ending part of the work of an apostle.

John says, *'I have much to write to you, but I do not want to do so with pen and ink. I hope to see you soon, and we will talk face to face* (3 Jn.13-14).

Nevertheless, John did pick up his pen and ink and write a letter, because something needed to be communicated immediately - in this instance, to his friend, Gaius. It couldn't wait for a later visit; Gaius had to be written to, then and there!

We can sense that Paul, also, had pressing moments, when he knew that he had to communicate something quickly! The first letter to the Thessalonians reveals one of those occasions. Paul tells them, *'When we could stand it no longer...we sent Timothy... to strengthen and encourage you...When I could stand it no longer, I sent, to find out about your faith'* (1 Thess.3:1-5).

Paul, himself, had found it necessary to stay in Athens, but he was so stirred up, because of the urgency of the prompt within him, that he immediately sent Timothy off to visit the

Thessalonians. In the context of this passage, Timothy's return with good news, then prompts Paul to send off the letter we now call First Thessalonians (1 Thess.3:6). When he did this, I don't think it was a case of just sticking a stamp on an envelope! I suspect a messenger will have taken the letter, involving even more communication. Finally, when the letter arrived, the church read that Paul was urging them to make sure it was *'read to all the brothers'* (1 Thess.5:27). He wanted its contents fully communicated to everyone!

Like John and Paul, apostles should be alert to the importance of maintaining communications across the territory assigned to them, and this should be an encouragement to all of us to do the same.

## THE HUMAN CONNECTION

In all their communications, apostles are building relationships with those around them. Whatever work is happening, it is being done in the context of relationships, and so, their communications are reflecting that. Therefore, an acknowledgement of our humanity, even on a very basic level, is important in all our communications. We are social creatures, born into a setting with a growing circle of relationships. There are personal events going on in our lives – people are unwell, family members are getting married, children are being born. Everyone is special and precious to God, and so our communications should keep that thought in mind. What a contrast there is between an email or a telephone call, where someone asks you how you are, and how your family are; as opposed to someone just writing your name, before wading straight in to their message, and thereby missing a great opportunity to build relationships!

## GREETINGS

When we write a letter or message to greet someone and say, 'Hello', we have the opportunity to establish and build our relationship with them; to show them that they are loved and matter to us, and to God.   The underlying Greek word, *'aspazomai'*, translated *'to greet'* literally means, *'to draw to oneself'* and, in fact, sometimes gets translated as *'embrace'*.

There are a lot of greetings being shared in the letters of the New Testament. They go beyond a form of words, and show that the writers really cared for the people to whom they were writing. Paul, for example, wasn't ordering people around like pawns on a chess board. He starts his letter to the Colossian church with these words, *'To the holy and faithful brothers in Christ at Colosse – grace and peace to you from God our Father'* (Col.1:2). He recognised the human connections going on. In a single line, he conveys love, honour and vision; showing that the Colossians were precious believers, for whom he desired the best.

Paul knew that the network of relationships across the church, in an area, needed maintaining. So he not only sent his own greetings, but also took the opportunity to convey the greetings of others as well. For example, to the Colossian church, Paul writes, *'Our dear friend Luke the doctor, and Demas send their greetings'* (Col.4:14). Sometimes, he not only greeted a whole church generally, but also singled out particular people, for a special mention. At the end of the letter to the Romans, Paul's greetings reached new levels, when he greeted over twenty-five people by name, other groups as well! (Rom.16:3-16).

Apostles remind us to take our greetings to one another as serious opportunities to establish and build our relationships.

## NEWS

People need news. All the time we are making news and passing on news. News gets reported and spreads from one person to another! People are hearing things, good and bad. Unfortunately, sometimes, they are being misinformed, or hearing only half the story!

Paul is a good example of an apostle who is aware of the need to constantly keep people informed. He doesn't want any misunderstandings to happen. For example, he spends time carefully explaining his thinking to the Corinthian church, so that they can understand why he had not visited them, at the time they had expected.(2 Cor.1:15 - 2:4).

If he had not given them an explanation in this letter, it may have undermined their confidence in him. He knew that a letter, giving his reasons for not visiting, was needed

However, news wasn't always about heavy duty stuff! Tychicus, for example, was sent by Paul, along with a letter, as his trusted mouth-piece to the Ephesian church. Paul had confidence that Tychicus would let the Ephesians know all his news – all the little personal details of how he was doing.

*'Tychicus…will tell you everything so that you also may know how I am and what I am doing. I am sending him to you for this very purpose that you may know how we are…'* (Eph.6:21-22).

As Paul says in a letter sent to another church, *'Tychicus will tell you all the news…'* (Col.4:7-8). Paul had sent him, along with Onesimus, *'to tell you everything that is happening here'* (Col.4:9). Tychicus was clearly a wonderful communicator!

Apostles encourage us to communicate well, so that we understand what is happening in the lives of those we are concerned about, as well as keeping them up to date with our news.

## REPORTS AND EVIDENCE

Sometimes there is a more serious edge to Paul's communications. When Paul and Barnabas returned to Antioch, from their first mission trip, they reported back to the church *'all that God had done through them'* (Acts 14:27).

They had been sent out from Antioch, and now they were sharing with them a good report of the outcome.

When Paul arrived in Rome, (Acts 21:19) he *'reported in detail what God had done among the gentiles through his ministry'* As far as we are aware, he had not been to Rome before, and felt the need to explain to the people there, what he had been doing before his arrival.

When Paul and Barnabas were appointed to go to Jerusalem, to sort out questions about the new gentile believers, they *'reported everything God had done through them'* (Acts 15:4). This was part of the evidence that they presented to the council in Jerusalem - that God was indeed at work among the gentiles. After the council had finished, they returned to Antioch with other chosen men to report about the decisions that had been reached by the council (Acts 15:22). Paul then made return visits to all the churches which had been established earlier, to see how they were doing (Acts 15:36), and *'as they travelled from town to town, they delivered the decisions reached at Jerusalem'* (Acts 16:4).

All these more official reports are part of good communications, which help others to trust in the character and ministry of an apostle.

## COMMUNICATING ARRANGEMENTS

In the New Testament letters, we also see that apostles were involved with some business-like arrangements. For example, Paul made arrangements for the carrying of an offering to Jerusalem. He wrote careful instructions about what to do with the offering, and who was to take it. Paul was ensuring that good communications were being maintained, and that everything was seen to be done right (2 Cor.8:21). Elsewhere, it is mentioned that he would write letters of introduction for those who were carrying the offering (1 Cor.16:3).

# LETTERS OF RECOMMENDATION

In some circumstances, letters of recommendation were clearly part of the communications that were expected. In the case of the Corinthian church, Paul protested that surely he didn't need such things from them, or to them, as some might have required! (2 Cor.3:1). However, Paul himself, wrote letters of commendation for others, from time to time. Here is an example, *'I commend to you our sister, Phoebe, a deaconess of the church in Cenchrea. I ask you to receive her in the Lord in a way worthy of the saints and to give her any help she may need from you, for she has been a great help to many people, including me'* (Rom.16:1-2).

We also read in Acts that Priscilla and Aquila wrote a letter of introduction for Apollos, when he went off for his first teaching visit to Corinth (Acts 18:27). It was helpful for the churches, receiving a new person, to know something about their character, as well as who sent them and where they were coming from. In this way the apostles provided reassurance that visiting believers were to be trusted.

# TRAVEL HELP

Sometimes letters needed to be written to sort out travel arrangements; such as, when Paul was passing through an area, and needed somewhere to stay. He writes to the Christians in Rome, *'When I go to Spain, I hope to visit you while passing through and have you assist me on my journey there'* (Rom.15:24).

On other occasions, he had to make arrangements to stay over winter, particularly when sailing was obviously not a good idea!

Paul always kept people posted about his intentions. For example to Titus, he wrote, *'As soon as I send Artemas or Tychicus to you, do your best to come to me at Nicopolis because I have decided to winter there'* (Tit.3:12). He went on to ask him, *'do everything you can to help Zenas the lawyer and Apollos on their way and see that they have everything they need'* (Tit.3:13). To the Corinthian church, he wrote regarding Timothy, that they *'send him on his way in peace so that he may return to me'* (1 Cor.16:11).

## OUR EXPERIENCE

Mary and I spend a lot of time connecting with people, either individually, or in gatherings and forums. Relationships have been built over cups of coffee, emails and telephone calls. Like everyone else, since the covid-19 pandemic, we have been learning to use zoom, and our travelling has been considerably reduced, as a result!

Over the years we have brought people together from across the church spectrum around mission projects, and in worship and prayer. We have given teaching input and hosted workshops. A lot of communication has been needed to do this successfully. We have had to show care and consideration for the different ones taking part, and have tried to understand where they were coming from church-wise, so we could adjust the manner and language used in our communications.

When we have arrived as newcomers into a city or a region, we have always felt it was important to come with humility. Others may have been labouring in that place for years, and there will be much for us to learn from them. No-one wants to meet someone with a 'we have arrived' attitude! Over cups of coffee and lunchtime meals, we have deliberately popped up in the lives of people who have been actively working on the ground. By starting with a lot of listening, we usually find God highlighting the things He is already doing in an area. Through building friendships, we have then spent a lot of time and effort encouraging the wider, joined-up thinking already taking place, as well as identifying some new projects to do.

There has been no grand over-arching plan, no posturing or empire building – we have been digging burrows of connection where they were needed, and learning how to communicate better, in order to see God's plans coming about! For example, in our local town, this connecting enabled us to begin a regular worship event across the church, called Open Wells. The planning team involved two other couples, whom we had met through our connecting work.

Another example of a new project coming about through our connecting work, is a regional prayer net; this required a lot of connecting work in order to develop it. The idea was to encourage all the prayers across the region, to come together in prayer. For our first event, dispersed prayer groups prayed in and around the same weekend. They were scattered geographically, but together, formed a common net of prayer. Over time, relationships have been built and strengthened, and a planning group formed. This has resulted in some more recent events via zoom, where Christians have prayed regionally, for healthy church and effective mission.

We have seen good communications helping to nurture and encourage the purposes of God in our particular region.

# CHAPTER ELEVEN
## ENCOURAGEMENT
## AND SUPPORT

*Apostles bring helpful words, which wake people up to God's purposes and plans. As a result, barren or stalled situations become fruitful, as people reconnect with whom they are meant to be.*

*Gophers - God's words of life change things - Encouraged by sharing experiences - Releasing people, giving permission - Encouragement and practical help - Waking up, starting again - Remind and recall - Releasing a new atmosphere - Resetting culture - Investing in people - Enlarged hearts - Labourers in the market place - Bringing overview and strategy - Identifying and resourcing - A changing environment - Re-imagining church - Paul's example of encouragement - Mutual support - Mutual encouragement*

## GOPHERS

It was after a prayer breakfast; I was sitting down having a conversation with a friend, when the subject of gophers came up. My friend began to talk about the eruption of Mount St. Helen's in Washington state, on the 16th May 1980. The eruption of this long-dormant volcano had caused complete devastation of the landscape for miles around it. In the immediate aftermath, the area took on the appearance of a moonscape! People assumed that the vegetation around the volcano would take years to recover, but it actually sprouted up quite rapidly! Scientists were at first surprised, and then, later, concluded that this was largely due to the activities of gophers.

During the eruption, these small furry animals had hidden underground; but, afterwards, as they burrowed their way up to the surface, unintentionally they brought up seeds with them. As a result, new growth was sprouting up at a much faster rate than anyone had expected. As the gophers had 'popped up' to the surface, they had brought new life and fruitfulness to an otherwise barren situation. When I heard my friend describing this, I knew that God was speaking to me about more than just gophers. So I listened carefully to try to understand what this picture, of yet another underground animal, might have to say to me.

## GOD'S WORDS OF LIFE CHANGE THINGS

What the gophers had done, in the landscape around the volcano, illustrates perfectly how God can use apostles to bring encouragement and change. The gophers had popped up to the surface, bringing life-giving seeds with them. By doing this, their activity had radically changed the appearance of the area, bringing amazing fruitfulness that had seemed impossible.

Similarly, apostles can bring change to the landscape, into which they are sent. They pop up, in places and in people's lives, and, as they do so, they bring God's words of life, which make all the difference.

## ENCOURAGED BY SHARING EXPERIENCES

When God wants to encourage and strengthen something which is already happening in a particular location, He will often send an apostle, to bring specific words, through teaching, or in conversation, which will do just that. The experiences shared by the apostle are, quite often, a perfect fit for the situation, and become encouraging examples, from which, the people living in that place can gain wisdom. Their situation may have felt discouraging, but now they see that God hasn't left them alone after all! He has sent someone, who has been through a similar set of experiences to what they are now going through, in order to show them some practical steps forward. The words of advice, brought by the apostle, come with authenticity and authority, because they have come at the cost of his own experience.

For example, many years ago, Bob and I established a Christian school. We have also had periods of time when we were home-educating our family of seven children. So that's a lot of education to have been involved in! Over a number of years, I have taught each one of our children, in turn, their ABC's, and experienced the wonder of seeing them beginning to read and write, after just a few weeks! These experiences have very ably equipped us to encourage other parents, who have recently been considering doing something similar.

Other areas in which we have also had personal experience in the past are church planting, and engaging with the cultural diversity in our town, city or region. So, more recently, Bob and I have been able to pop up and encourage others, through conversations with pastors in the early stages of church planting, or when we've provided teaching to churches on how to engage with the cultural diversity of their area. In some other instances, we have simply signposted people to helpful resources, or connecting them with good creative ideas elsewhere. Even if our own experiences haven't been directly helpful, we have often known someone else who could help and advise them.

Whether in prayer, teaching input or conversations, God often uses the experiences of an apostle as a helpful sounding board for others.

## RELEASING PEOPLE – GIVING PERMISSION

On many occasions, the work of an apostle is to help release and launch someone, into the calling that God has for their lives. Fear may have kept them back, or wrong thinking that somehow they weren't properly qualified. The apostle, in just a short conversation, can be the impetus for them to step out on a new adventure! All the gifting and means were already there, in them – they just needed the cork to be taken out of the bottle, and for the new things to flow out and begin. It's as if they needed someone to give them permission to get going!

An apostle can give someone the sense of validation that they need. They may have been sitting on their gifting, struggling to venture onto new ground, but then, from a short conversation, suddenly they can feel released - re-awakened to their purpose and ready to _gopher_ it (Ouch! I couldn't resist the word-play!).

## ENCOURAGEMENT AND PRACTICAL HELP

With certain people the blockage preventing them from

stepping into their calling may not be fear of change, but simply that they just don't know <u>how</u> to get there. They may have sat on a God-given dream or vision for years, because they didn't know the practicalities of how to do it.

A few years ago, for example, it was a real joy, for Bob and I to come alongside a friend and encourage her to follow through her vision for starting an art group (called God's Artwork) The idea was for a few creative friends to meet in a café, prayerfully wait on God, draw, colour, or create pictures, and share their finished work, as a gift, with the customers. It needed a café owner who was sympathetic to the cause, and also willing to give them permission.

As this lady stepped out into her ministry, it has been a blessing to so many, to receive pictures which were literally 'a gift from God'. Our friend had been thinking of doing this for many years, but hadn't quite got there with it. A little bit of encouragement from us, and help in setting up a bank account, and she was off!

## WAKING UP – STARTING AGAIN

As in this example here, apostles can help people to work through how to start again, in an effective and relevant way, by acting as a sounding board for them.

Every so often, Bob and I meet up with someone, whom we have known well in the past. As we chat with them, we begin to realise that something that was working well for them, in their ministry, now needs reviving and reconnecting - it has gone dormant! They may talk about feeling that they have gone to sleep on the things that got them excited in the past.
It seems to be a stalled situation – as if the tools have been laid down, scattered and forgotten.

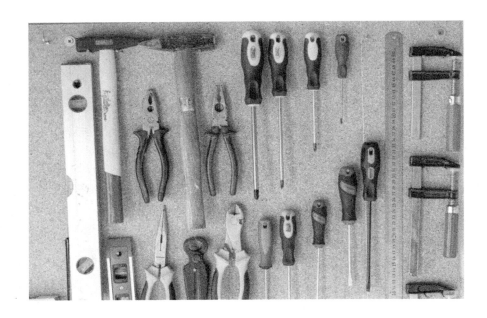

Suddenly, however, in the context of a single conversation with ourselves, they can be re-awakened to the task! The tools are picked up again, and put in the toolbox ready for active use. Good things start again; things that had been happening, but had stopped for a season. The seed is stirred up once more, and prayers, prayed long ago, come up with fresh effect. Fresh hope has come, as God has used our words to encourage and wake someone up, simply in conversation with them.

## REMIND AND RECALL

Apostles help to remind us of who we are in Christ, and of the noble task in which we are engaged. They prompt us to recall the words spoken to us in the past, which have helped us to live our lives in ways that please God. As Peter writes,
*'I have written both of [my letters] as <u>reminders</u> to stimulate you to wholesome thinking. I want you to <u>recall</u> the words spoken in the past by the holy prophets and the command given by our Lord and Saviour through your apostles'* (2 Pet.3:1-2).

Jesus told the first disciples that they were His friends, because he was sharing with them everything that the Father had shared with him (Jn.15:15). He also knew how easy it was for them to forget things, and so he reassured them that the Holy Spirit would be there as well, to remind them of everything that he had said to them (Jn.14:26).

However, the Holy Spirit is given to all of us, who are believers; as John wrote, *'all of you know the truth'*, and *'the anointing you received...remains in you, and you do not need anyone to teach you...'* (1 Jn.2:20, 27).

This doesn't mean that we won't forget the things we have been taught! Even though the Spirit can speak to us directly, He will often use other people to remind us of the words that God has spoken to us.
Like Peter, in his letter (2Pet 3:1-2), apostles recognise that we have a need to recall the good things which have kept us on track – the words from God, spoken over us, and so they will intentionally want to remind us of them.

## RELEASING A NEW ATMOSPHERE

Apostles have an initiating role in releasing a different spiritual atmosphere into an area. By faith, they declare new things that currently are not, as though they are. They sense that God is at work, in a bigger way, causing a shift in the culture, and so they aim to flow along with what they believe He is doing. Their aim is to encourage, in people, the heart attitudes which will nurture revival.

In big and small settings, they come along, and begin to create an environment where people are released into their purpose; like boats being untied along the quayside, to set off on their journeys. (Some ways in which apostles do this, are discussed in the rest of this chapter.)

It doesn't end there, however; having untied the boats, apostles then help to navigate people, to where they really want to go. The overall effect is a significant change in the atmosphere.

## RESETTING CULTURE

One thing about small animals is that they can get into places larger ones can't! Even spiders, (or lizards, depending on your translation) are found in King's palaces! (Prov.30:28). God can open up all kinds of opportunities to those who come with a humble, non-threatening attitude. A gentle manner and the integrity to keep confidences, for example, can disarm the political great, in a single strategic conversation. This is one way in which apostles may help change the atmosphere.

Another way might be much more public, and require apostles to obstinately and persistently lobby for a righteous viewpoint to be upheld. However, whether in loud or quiet ways, the activities of apostles can be used by God to re-set the culture. Of course, and very importantly, a lot of prayer will have been part of the process as well.

## INVESTING IN PEOPLE

Local churches may often evaluate the people in their congregations in terms of what they can do to help the church. This kind of thinking tends to squash people's dreams and gifts. God wants people to be invested in, equipped and developed. He doesn't want them hung out to dry, because the church doesn't know how to include them in their weekly programme. It would be much better if the church saw herself as a place to equip and facilitate others, in what they are doing, out in the community; in the market place, in schools and where they live.

Apostles can help shift this huge problem in mindsets. The job of the apostle, in this instance, is aptly described by Isaiah chapter fifty-four, as a call to, *'Enlarge the place of your tent, stretch your tent curtains wide, do not hold back, lengthen your cords, strengthen your stakes'* (Isa.54:2).

Apostles are calling out for a more generous, wider mindset from local churches; to think bigger than their own arena. This will also change the spiritual atmosphere of an area.

## ENLARGED HEARTS

Young people coming back into a local church, from a year-out experience, such as with YWAM, or new people moving into an area, also need to be encouraged in how God might want to use them within the church, or in the community. Apostles can help to change the receiving atmosphere of the church, so that the gifts people bring are released and used properly.

Of course, there is also a need for those returning to church to show humility, wisdom and honour towards others already present. No-one wants a 'brand', or church style, from elsewhere forced down their throats! The faithful labours of many, who have been working in an area for years, mustn't be disregarded. However, if you are a newcomer to the area, don't be intimidated into feeling that you are not allowed to make a difference there for the Kingdom of God. Arriving in the area at a later stage than others, doesn't disqualify you! It is good to honour those who have worked hard, in the heat of the day, but know that God has called you to contribute something important, as well. Each of us must follow the wind of the Spirit in whatever fresh direction He is leading us! (Jn.3:8).

# LABOURERS IN THE MARKET PLACE

The parable of the hired labourers, in Matthew chapter twenty, tells how a farmer went down to the market place to hire labourers, at different times throughout the whole day. He was even hiring workers at the eleventh hour, which sounds pretty late to me! I can imagine the labourers hired earlier, saying, *'What are you doing here? Why bother? The job is nearly done'*. However, the farmer hired them all. (Mt. 20:1-16). They were all needed, not just the ones who began the work, but also those who arrived later!

Apostles encourage a renewed generosity of spirit, and enlarged hearts among those already at work in an area. This was Paul's plea to the Corinthians, *'Open wide your hearts'* (2 Cor.6:13). He had come to them in an open-hearted manner; and modelled the heart change he wanted to see in them. Now it was their turn to respond in a similar manner.

## BRINGING OVERVIEW AND STRATEGY

We all need to appreciate the wider perspective of what the Lord is doing across the whole church in a region.

Apostles bring overview and strategy. They understand the bigger picture, of God's plans and purposes in a region, or in a nation. This helps people to see what they are doing, in the details of their lives, with a new perspective; how we all fit together as pieces of the jigsaw puzzle. Apostles help to nurture healthy relationships, and joined up thinking. They invite us to see our area from God's heavenly viewpoint; with fresh eyes, beyond the bricks and mortar of everyday life. So, we start to feel encouraged that God is at work in our region, and that the words 'I will build my church' are true, just as Jesus promised. Apostles remind us that we are in a harvest field, and the Lord of the Harvest has a harvest plan.

In our region, for example, there is a shifting to a wider understanding of what leadership might look like, away from a professional clergy. Formerly, clergy would have been expected to exclusively assume the leadership role. Mary and I, in our part of the harvest field, are encouraging a much wider definition of leadership. Our heart is that those involved in creative ways of doing mission, should hear from one another, across the whole spectrum of church, whether they have a formal label or not. Good cross-fertilisation can then take place, as people hear good news stories of what is happening in the wider context, and are then able to share their own stories, and pray for one another.

Alongside this, we also believe it is God's strategy for the prayers, the worshippers and the prophetic to find one another in this wider context. Out of a heavenly place of intimacy, we have enjoyed seeing these groups of believers coming together, and flowing in the Spirit in a powerful synergy.

Mary and I have been creating opportunities, for those from these three groups, of whom we are aware, to meet up. We believe that their coming together is nurturing and encouraging revival. It is all about relationships! For example, as part of this strategy, we have helped to host worship workshops, which encourage relationship, and worship creativity, between worship teams in our area. Of course, many others are also at work, in different ways, in our region and it is important to honour how God is working in all of them. He is mobilising His people beyond our imagination, in whatever way He chooses. We are just a part of what He is doing.

## IDENTIFYING AND RESOURCING

An overview of a region, or nation, identifies the spiritual and other needs of the communities. It also reveals the strengths and the weaknesses in how the church, as a whole, is functioning in these communities. As apostles listen, and are led by the Holy Spirit, they can help identify what is lacking, and establish ministry projects which will address it. Their wider over-view can inform the local Christians, and also connect resources and experience from elsewhere, for the encouragement and benefit of all.

In one borough in London, for instance, Mary and I were able to use information and help about how to start up a food bank, which was available nationally, to initiate one locally. We did something similar with Healing on the Streets, making use of national training and experience to establish a local project.

## A CHANGING ENVIRONMENT

The spiritual landscape, being overviewed by apostles, is a constantly changing one! We are aware of one ministry which invites church leaders to physically climb up to a high place or building, and look down at their communities. They then spend time asking God to show them how it looks from His perspective. This is really helpful for bringing overview, and joined-up thinking, across the church. Leaders become aware that theirs is not the only church in the landscape; and that God is actually at work in the whole neighbourhood, much more than they may have realised.

However, as mentioned earlier, the spiritual landscape, which they are viewing, is a constantly changing one. If they look again, a year or so later, it may have changed dramatically! We have to accept that our maps and surveys will need revising, because we are dealing with a changing environment. The culture in which we all swim is constantly changing; people are on the move, or, if not, they are changing as they grow older!

No wonder that, in the Bible, the waves of the sea are a common symbol for the affairs of men. Waves are difficult to map! In this respect, if apostles are bringing overview, they are like pioneers who keep arriving in a territory that has never been mapped before. Even if others have been there before, their earlier descriptions of what they saw, will not tally with what a later apostle might now see. Our overviews are snapshot pictures of the wave movements of the moment. We cannot set them in concrete for all time, as if they are the final word on what God is doing.

We produced a film documentary called 'God on the Move', just four years ago, which appeared on Revelation TV. Its aim was to encourage believers that, indeed, God was on the move in their communities. We illustrated this with some wonderful examples of people and projects going on in Havering; one of the outer London boroughs. You can still see the film on Youtube, and for people elsewhere, it still serves its purpose, but, if you are from Havering, it looks like archive footage from another era. So much has changed in just four years!

## RE-IMAGINING CHURCH

Accepting that we are in a changing environment, opens us up to re-imagine the possibilities of what we might be doing in the future, in a changed setting.

At this present time, God has been stirring up Mary and I to rethink what church might look like. Our particular focus has been on how scattered believers can connect and encourage one another, and to think about mission in their area. Our own region contains both urban and rural elements. In the context of the rural, we have become aware of isolated and scattered pockets of folk – individuals, couples and small groups. These are those who don't fit easily into traditional church models, but nevertheless love Jesus, and want to reach their community with the gospel. Our desire has been to engage with, and encourage them. We have achieved this over the Lockdown period of 2020/2021, mainly via zoom meetings online. By networking together, in a wider context, these, mostly home-based, pockets of folk are now having fellowship and supporting mission together. A new wineskin has been developing as a result.

The way that church looks is being re-visited and re-imagined. A certain degree of experimentation is going on, and people are being stirred up to step out into the new adventure that God has for them.

## PAUL'S EXAMPLE OF ENCOURAGEMENT

The apostle Paul, understood that he had been given authority from God to build up, and not to tear down (2 Cor.10:8). In the context in which Paul wrote these words, he was expressing his longing that the Corinthian church might be encouraged and built up. Dramatic things had gone on in their lives. Everything they had been used to seeing as normal, in their lifestyles, was being challenged. Through the common work of the Holy Spirit, they had heard the gospel and suddenly, complete strangers had been thrown together, and were only just beginning to understand their unity as one body, with Christ as their head!

Paul's desire was to establish them and bring them to maturity. The church in Corinth had come into being through Paul's ministry of apostleship, in the first place.
*'Even though I might not be an apostle to others, surely I am to you! For you are the seal of my apostleship in the Lord'* (1 Cor.9:2).
They were Paul's baby, and his letters show an intense longing and affection for them. He wants to be a comfort to them and says, *'if we are distressed it is for your comfort and salvation, if we are comforted, it is for your comfort...'* (2 Cor.1:6).
It was a source of great grief to Paul when things were going wrong and he was forced to intervene. The last thing Paul wanted was to be a trouble to them. Paul's aim was always to encourage them. To another church, he wrote, *'I long to see you so that I may impart to you some spiritual gift to make you strong'* (Rom.1:11).

When Paul sends different ones to the churches, which he had helped to establish, it is with the express purpose of encouraging them. He sends Timothy, for example, to the Thessalonian church *'to strengthen and encourage'* them (1 Thess.3:2). Likewise, Tychicus is sent to the church in Ephesus to encourage the believers there (Eph.3:2).

Paul is a good example for all apostles; that they are there, to

encourage other believers. In every situation, he wants his words to build people up. In letter after letter, written by Paul, we see that he was following his own maxim,
*'Do not let any unwholesome talk come out of your mouths, but only what is helpful for building others up according to their needs, that it may benefit those who listen'* (Eph.4:29).

His letters are a testimony to his constant concern for the churches, that they should be built up and encouraged.
*'Besides everything else, I face daily the pressure of my concern for all the churches'* (2Cor.11:28).
They were always in his thoughts.

## MUTUAL SUPPORT

Apostles also stir up a mutual giving and receiving of support and encouragement between believers. We have already read how Paul was involved in organising a collection of money from the churches, for the saints in Jerusalem, and also how he would write on behalf of others, such as Phoebe, in his letter to the church in Rome (Rom.16:1). He was consistently stirring up the churches to support one another, and also to pray and give support, to those on ministry assignments elsewhere.

Paul, himself, was a recipient of support from other believers, as well. To the Corinthian church, he said, *'the brothers who came from Macedonia supplied what I needed'* (2 Cor.11:9).
He wrote of the Philippians that *'in Thessalonica, you sent me aid, again and again, when I was in need'* (Phil.4:16).
The Philippians even sent him Epaphroditus - *'whom you sent to take care of my needs'* (Phil.2:25).

In this passage, in Philippians, is an interesting use of the word 'apostle', as Paul describes Epaphroditus as *their apostle.* He had been sent by them, with their full authority and backing, to be for Paul, exactly what they would have been, if they had been there themselves. Hence the term 'apostle' is used. Similarly, those sent by the churches with the money collection, for the saints in Jerusalem, are described as *apostles*, because they were being sent with their authority as representatives. (this is how the NIV translates *'apostolos'* in 2Cor. 8:23). These references do illustrate how broadly the word, apostle, can be used; and should send a warning shot to anyone trying to limit its definition in the New Testament.

## MUTUAL ENCOURAGEMENT

Paul also received encouragement, as well as giving it, just by hearing news from the churches. For example, he was comforted by the coming of Titus from the church in Corinth (2 Cor.7:6). Again, Timothy was sent to the Philippians, knowing that Paul would be cheered up by receiving news from them. Paul lets them know that he wanted their encouragement (Phil.2:19). On another occasion, he tells Timothy that he longs to see him, so that he might be filled with joy (2 Tim.1:4). In this way, Timothy is being stirred up, by Paul, to come, ready with that encouragement that Paul needed.

Paul understood that his interactions with other believers would be a source of mutual encouragement. They needed to know that they were as much a blessing to him, as he was to them: and so, he stirs them up accordingly. For example, to the Roman church, he says, *'I long to see you...that you and I may be mutually encouraged by each other's faith'* (Rom.1:12). Towards the end of the same letter, he says, *'Pray...that I may come to you with joy, and together with you be refreshed'* (Rom.15:32).

Support and encouragement are an essential part of the building up and maturing process. As Paul writes in Ephesians, chapter four, *'From [Christ] the whole body joined and* *held together by every supporting ligament grows and <u>builds itself</u> <u>up</u> in love, <u>as each part does its work</u>'* (Eph.4:16).

Like Paul, apostles today, are stirring up each part of the body of Christ to do its bit, to encourage and build up the whole.

**Who can you support and encourage today?**

# CHAPTER TWELVE
## DISTURBING AND DISRUPTING

*One role of apostles is to disturb. They disturb old paradigms. They go in and break things up that have lost their relevancy. When things have lost their point, something needs to be done. Apostles make adjustments; they characteristically come in and break down any walls of religion, that have built up in the life of the church.*

*Moles – Routines and bad habits - Breaking down bad thinking - Wrong competitive thinking - Wrong complimentary thinking - Collaborative thinking*

## MOLES

I was sitting in a country graveyard one day and suddenly had a thought about how very disturbing it would be, for the relatives of those buried there, if the graveyard was covered in molehills! No-one wants the remains of their loved ones to be disturbed, and so, I couldn't imagine that moles would be very welcome in a graveyard.

Just a short while before this, Mary and I had received a word about moles. They had been highlighted to us, as we were listening to a lady speaking at a leader's prayer day, which we had organised, in one of the London boroughs. This was the third underground animal that God had highlighted for us to consider, in just as many months! We'd had three words in a row, rabbits, gophers and now, moles. However, it wasn't until I was sitting in that church yard a few months later that I realised it was their disturbing quality that God was particularly pointing out to us. I had been wondering, 'Why moles, Lord?, and now God was giving me an unexpected insight. Like moles in a graveyard, one difficult aspect which God sometimes calls apostles to do, is to break up the ground, disturbing the status quo.

## ROUTINES AND BAD HABITS

At first Mary and I, were not comfortable about what God might be saying, through this underground animal. We weren't very keen to disrupt anything! We were about to move to a new area, and didn't feel that this was something we really saw ourselves doing. However, we started to understand and accept that, if we were going to be popping up into people's lives, we might well find ourselves, on occasions, disturbing comfortable routines.

We all love our routines and can resent their disturbance, but most things swerve to rot, if left alone long enough. Bad habits which have built up over time, do need breaking. Church is no exception, and has a sad tendency to swerve towards manmade religiosity. What can start off as Holy Spirit-led spontaneity has the awful tendency of ending up being just another religious habit.

Routines can develop even over a very short time; and while you are in the middle of certain routines, they can have an ageless quality about them! Over the years, we have been to a number of Summer Christian camps. They generally start on a Saturday, and by Wednesday you feel as if you have been there forever! You know the neighbours in the tents next to you, and there is a pattern to the week which, by Wednesday, you are completely familiar and comfortable with. Shockingly, however, it does all come to a wonderful climax and end; and the re-adjustment afterwards can be very hard!

However much we know that we really can't stay on a Christian camp forever, its ending can be distressing. The very first camp we attended was on a showground in Malvern. We had car difficulties at the end of the camp, and limped along to a local garage, to get the car sorted out. Much later, as we drove back, we passed the showground, and found it very disturbing as we saw that the camp had all gone. What had been like heaven on earth for us, for a week, had vanished!

Routines are commendable as long as they are treated as a temporary, holding exercise. They should be the temporary scaffolding erected, to help things move forward at that moment; whether that moment is a week or a year.

## BREAKING DOWN BAD THINKING

As well as being used to disturb comfortable routines, apostles also help to break down bad thinking. The apostle, Paul, had authority to build up, rather than to tear down, but in the second letter to the Corinthians we discover that he is doing both! He is needing to firmly address poor moral behaviour in

*'How good and pleasant it is when brothers live together in unity!'* **(Ps.133:1).**

the Corinthian church, in order for a more godly life to emerge (see 2 Cor.10:8, 13:10). In other words; for the building up of the church to progress, a demolition work had to be carefully executed, at the same time. If you have seen films of buildings being demolished, you will recognise that it is an amazing skill to demolish something, without causing damage to the surrounding area.

Demolition is one option open to the apostle. However, on some occasions, it may be best to leave the tares and the wheat growing together, and just encourage the wheat to flourish. The old tares will take their own course, and in time may wither away. On the other hand they may not! Bad thinking may have to be challenged, and unlearnt, for a new mindset to emerge. It is important for apostles to listen to the Holy Spirit, so He can guide them to make the right call.

## WRONG COMPETITIVE THINKING

Competitive thinking between churches is a major issue that apostles have to address in the church. They, themselves, can be part of the problem, particularly if they are the ones heading up the churches! Their actions can easily be interpreted as being done for the advantage of their own church. Paul warned against a partisan spirit that gathers people to follow, but then assumes a position of superiority over other parts of the church. He addresses this issue, for example, in his letter to the Corinthian church, which had already split into factions - *'I follow Paul... I follow Apollos...I follow Cephas...I follow Christ'* (1 Cor.1:12).

This partisan thinking can be blatant, but is often quite subtle and indirect, because everyone knows that Christians are supposed to love another!

If we consider ourselves as <u>superior</u> custodians of the gospel, then we can feel justified at promoting ourselves above other inferior 'brands'. We might even suggest that these other groups are not proper churches at all! Suggestions can be made that, somehow, they are not sound doctrinally; or they are personality cults around a leader; or cowboy outfits, lacking proper governance and safeguards.

It is sad to see local church or regional denominations, busy with their own agenda without showing any interest in what others may be doing. Even worse, if they are keeping an eye on others in order to protect their own turf. Both older and newer church groups can fall foul of this narrow thinking. I remember being present in one denominational leaders meeting, where the closure of a church building was being lamented, and the departure of the minister to another church group, seen as a betrayal. The bigger kingdom picture wasn't being considered at all. The idea that the Holy Spirit might have been leading the minister in his decision, never came into the discussion.

One church group we know, has a policy to plant a church in every community. This sounds very commendable until you realise that this is a blanket policy, which makes no reference to what God might be doing through other churches, already situated in those communities. A church planter is sent out to start a new church, regardless of the activity of other churches already there.

In London, where suitable venues for churches are hard to find, sometimes, a community building will be shared by a number of churches. We know one sports centre where five churches meet each Sunday, sometimes concurrently. It can be hard to find the one you are looking for, within the building; but, as one church leader complained, it is much harder when one of the other church leaders keeps moving their rival's signage around, in a deliberate attempt to confuse people! This unbelievable behaviour was sadly true, and was probably part of a pattern of poor relationships between the different churches.

## WRONG COMPLEMENTARY THINKING

Complementary thinking about how to relate with other churches in a community, sounds much better, but has its own issues.

The idea of being complementary is that each church majors on its strengths, and allows the other churches in the area to serve in different areas of competence, without competition. So, one church may run a café, another a food bank and so on. One large church we knew began proactively relating with other churches in the area, and this was all very fine on one level. Communications had started, and relationships were beginning to develop. Then the leader of the large church said, to the other leaders, how they shouldn't be in competition with one another, and that their activities ought to complement each others. To this end, he had listed all the numerous activities in which his own church were engaged, and then invited the other smaller churches to offer what they could, to complement them! On that basis, they had nothing left to offer! Fortunately they stuck with the relationship, and later they were able to work together collaboratively on a number of projects, and honour one another, within that particular community.

In another city, the churches which met in their own buildings had held a cosy arrangement for years, where they took it in turns to host, and provide the preacher, at a Good Friday service, for all the other churches. This arrangement ignored, entirely, the presence of newer groups, which were meeting in schools and community centres. These groups just showed up, on the day, as 'also rans'. A simple change from one rota to two, one for the venue, and one for the preacher, was all that was needed to bring about a better arrangement, and thankfully, this was done. It wasn't difficult, but it required someone coming in, with a different perspective, to affect the change.

## COLLABORATIVE THINKING

The word that best expresses an understanding of the deeper unity, that apostles desire churches to have with one another, must be the word 'collaborative'.

The Lausanne statement says, '*It takes the whole church to take the whole gospel to the whole city*'. This requires a shift from both competitive and complementary thinking, to one of collaboration. Apostles can encourage this kind of mindset among the churches in an area, however the language of collaboration may well jar on some of them, and be an unwelcome disturbance. So it may not be possible for all the churches to come into agreement.

Apostles shouldn't think everything must be collaborative, however! There are some things which should remain distinctive. For example, if the Lord has given someone a particular mandate to pursue, who can argue? Vague gestures of unity should not be used to limit someone in their calling.

There are two questions, apostolic in nature, which need to be asked:-

'*What missional things can we do together which will reach the area?*'

'*How far are we willing to build relationships with other Christians?*'

Apostles help to build relationships across the wider church, by challenging bad habits and routines, and wrong ways of thinking. But, in the final analysis, it is the Lord, who very carefully examines the heart attitudes of each one of us. His desire is that everything should be done in a spirit of love and honour.

# CHAPTER THIRTEEN
## HIDDEN TREASURE

*God uses apostles to bring people out of darkness, like hidden treasure and wonderful jewels, to use for His glory.*

*Dug up by Jesus - A treasure found in God - A mining operation Twelve precious jewels - Treasures of Britain - Moles find treasure - Under our very noses*

**'I will give you hidden treasures; riches stored in secret places so that you may know that I am the LORD, the God of Israel who summons you by name' (Isa.45:3).**

This promise was given to Cyrus, the King of Persia (Isaiah chapters, 44 and 45), whose description we have previously read about in Chapter 5 of this book. He was fulfilling the role of an apostle, sent with God's authority, to accomplish all that God pleased, and God promised him that he would receive hidden treasures.

## A TREASURE FOUND IN GOD

You have to have your eye on the prize to think that it is worthwhile to go down into the depths of the earth, in order to find hidden treasure in the rocks! Job, chapter twenty-eight, gives us a picture of the diligent madness of the mining enterprise, in the secret places, far away from the activities of normal life! *'Far from where people dwell he cuts a shaft...he dangles and sways...he assaults the flinty rock...he tunnels...his eyes see all its treasures...he brings hidden things to light'* (Job 28:1-11).

The context of this passage in Job, is about wisdom only being found in God; he makes his point that no amount of mining will find what only God can give. The *'riches stored in secret places,'* promised to Cyrus, can only be found in God.

# DUG UP BY JESUS

When the jewels, being mined, are brought up to the surface, one imagines that the rejoicing would be on a par with the man, in the parable that Jesus told (Mt.13:44). This man sold everything he had, in order to buy the treasure which he had found, hidden in a field. Jesus said that this is what the Kingdom of God is like. Some people think that the parable is a picture of how *we* discover the kingdom, but others believe it is about Jesus, giving up everything, in order to have the treasure he had found. He came into the world to seek and to save what was lost (Lk.19:10). He looked for the treasure, and found us. He went into the darkness, shining a light, bringing us out, eyes blinking into his glorious light! In this understanding of the parable, the people of God are the treasure, once hidden in darkness, but now found by Jesus.

# A MINING OPERATION

Just like the kind of treasure promised to Cyrus, this treasure can only be given by the LORD. *'Apart from me, you can do nothing'*, says Jesus (John 15:5).

Apostles are like miners, recruited as part of a Holy Spirit mining operation, to bring out into the light, a people dwelling in darkness. Only in the power of God can they do this. This is why, after the ascension of Jesus, the apostles were told to wait until the Holy Spirit came upon them; they needed to be filled with His power in order to unearth the treasure (Acts 1:8).

One role of apostles is to release people caught up in the darkness and grip of the enemy. In the words used to describe Cyrus; the LORD takes hold of their right hands *'to subdue nations...and to strip kings of their armour'* (Isa.45:1).

As a result doors are opened before them, the gates of bronze are broken down, and people are brought out of captivity, to come home to the family of God. Of course, what Cyrus actually decreed historically (Ezr.1:1-4), is a foreshadowing of what Jesus has done. Jesus, in his authority as *the apostle* and high priest (Heb.3:1), has issued a decree, and sent out his apostles, to break open the ground and release the people.

## TWELVE PRECIOUS JEWELS

The LORD sees His people as precious jewels. For example, the ephod of the high priest in Israel carried a breast-piece, set with twelve different, precious jewels, representing the tribes of the people of God. Each jewel had once been a hidden treasure that had been found, cut and polished. What had once been in darkness, was now displayed in all its glory, on the high priest's breast-piece.

This is also the language used to describe the New Jerusalem - the Bride dressed for her husband. In John's vision, the New Jerusalem *'shone with the glory of God, and its brilliance was like that of a very precious jewel, like a jasper, clear as crystal'* (Rev.21:11). This amazing passage then describes the twelve foundations of the city wall, on which were written *'the names of the twelve apostles of the Lamb'*. The twelve foundations are described as twelve different precious jewels.

In a wonderful way, akin to John's vision of the heavenly bride as a city, Jesus our great High priest wears His Bride close to his heart as a breast-piece of jewels, shining with all His glory!

## TREASURES OF BRITAIN

Every person is valued and precious to God – a royal jewel, cut carefully, in order to shine in many different directions and looking altogether lovely. When apostles declare the rule of God in the areas to which they have been sent, they play their part in bringing these treasures out from the ground.

On my shelf at home is an old book from my sixties childhood, called 'Treasures of Britain'. It assembles in one volume a catalogue of the rich heritage of the British Isles, showing the places one can visit - castles, stately homes, ancient cathedrals and the birth-places of famous people. It is full of fantastic photos of paintings from art galleries and, of course, the crown jewels. There is a map section too, (with hardly a motorway on it, because few had been built in the sixties) so you can discover where these places are. One day, I felt God highlighting this book to me, as a picture of another 'Treasures of Britain' book that God has published for our land. This book is a heavenly book, detailing all the rich treasure of people, old and new, that He has here in Britain.

They are hidden in His heavenly treasure chest, waiting to be brought out. I felt the LORD say of the British Isles, *'I have My treasure in this place'*; and that looking to His ancient paths would find them. Jeremiah 6:16 came to my mind, as I looked at the old road map of Britain and Ireland in my book,
*'Stand at the crossroads and look; ask for the ancient paths, ask where the good way is and walk in it, and you will find rest for your souls...'*. The ancient paths are God's way for our lives. As we follow Jesus, we will find the treasure of people, hidden in the British Isles, and bring them into the light.

# MOLES FIND TREASURE

After all this grand talk of treasure and jewels, it seems strange to return to the subject of moles, but they are more appropriate to consider, in this connection, than one might think! All over the British Isles, moles are tunnelling and making their molehills, bringing up to the surface not just earth, but hidden treasure as well!

Last year, for example, someone found a medieval ring sitting on top of a molehill in their garden! Elsewhere, in our area, a team of volunteers carefully sieved their way through hundreds of molehills, on the site of a Roman fort, and pieced together all sorts of information about the fort, from the treasure which they had found. Part of a luxury bronze tap, shaped like a dolphin, for example, was just lying there, on the side of a molehill. The moles hadn't heard about any of the rules and regulations around excavations, and had just got on with their digging! As one BBC reporter said, *'Only the moles know the true extent of the fort's treasures'*. They had gone ahead and unearthed what others couldn't see!

## UNDER OUR VERY NOSES

From the perspective of the apostle, moles are an encouragement to us to believe that there is treasure, in the form of people, under our very noses! Moles are very local; they tunnel around in their own limited patch. We feel that God is prompting apostles to discover the people right in front of them – the jewels who are ready to be picked up and put into their proper place, in the new ventures, which God is revealing to us. Some of these people will find their place, and work alongside apostles, as our team.

# Hidden Treasure

Cleaning, polishing and restoring;
God sees the hidden treasure in us,
Others may only see rubbish
But He is the antique guy-
He sees what is hidden.

When the enemy tells you, "You're worthless!"
God looks inside you and sees hidden treasure.
When you put Him on the throne of your life,
He'll help you to overcome your past,
Resist temptation,
Break through your self-imposed limitations,
And start accepting that
In His eyes, you have great worth.

The divine nature is in me!
I am someone who is being transformed
Into His likeness.
I am an item that just needs to be cleaned,
Polished and restored,
In order to become valuable again.

(Matthew 13:44- hidden treasure; 2 Corinthians.3:18 - we are being transformed)

Mary Bain July 2008

# CHAPTER FOURTEEN
## TEAM

*We are all in a team of God's choosing. There are people whom God has called to be team with us, just as there are others, to whom He calls us, to be part of their team. God doesn't want apostles to work alone, but with others, in the territories assigned to them. We should expect to see teams emerging around us.*

*Our experience - Team is needed - Getting teams started - Male and female perspectives - A company of women - An army of grandmothers - The mighty men who help us - A team comes together - Raw materials - A quality team - Mutual help - Visionary names - Woven Together – Partnerships - New things*

## OUR EXPERIENCE

Even before, we arrived in the North East of England, God was going ahead and making connections for us, which would become team for us (or us, team for them). A year before we moved, we took a twenty-four hour trip up to Northumberland, to hear what God might be saying to us. Rather than us listening to God at a distance, we wanted our feet on the ground. We found ourselves in the centre of Newcastle, a major regional city there, and as we were coming out of a shop, we heard people worshipping. It was a group of four people involved in a ministry called Worship on the Streets. That day, they had decided to worship in a different place from their normal one. They had also continued worshipping for longer than usual! God had set us up to meet one another! We joined in, and then afterwards, we prayed together, and they gave us some significant prophetic words. Later that day, we went to an encouraging, worship and prophetic gathering which they had told us about; we were given even more prayer and prophetic words! From this twenty-four hour period, we felt that God had reassured us that whatever we decided, and wherever we ended up, there would be friends for us in our new destination. The four people in the worship group, whom we met that day, are all now significantly involved in what we are doing.

## TEAM IS NEEDED

Since our arrival in the North East, Mary and I have been trying to encourage worshippers, prayers and prophetic people across the area to connect together; in order to nurture and encourage revival. We are also encouraging people to be creative, in the way that they are doing mission. And we are helping to connect certain pockets of individuals, couples and groups, so that they can strengthen and support each other. These things can't be done alone, or in isolation, so we partner with others in teams, to plan and to do things. This makes us more effective and accurate in what we do. It is so true that *'just as iron sharpens iron, so one man sharpens another'* (Pr.27:17).

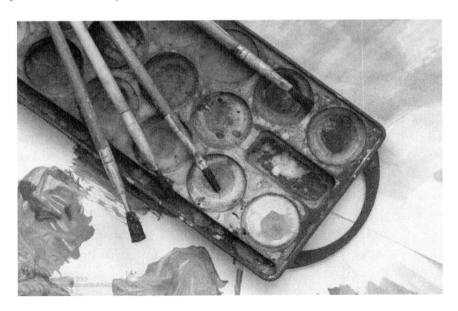

We are more likely to hear the mind of the Lord, as we bring our different personalities to the table. When a rich palette of paints is gathered together, wonderful paintings can start to happen!

## GETTING TEAMS STARTED

The presence of apostles will always help to get teams started. God once highlighted to us a photo on the wall of a village hall - young scouts were propping one another up, in a circle. Each scout was held and supported by the others. If we had been able to go back to the moment just before the photo, we would no doubt have seen that someone had helped them to line up into that position. This is how it is with the formation of teams; sometimes they are just waiting for the signal to come into line! Apostles listen up to those trumpet calls from heaven, that signal a change is happening, and they start to get the ball rolling, so the team can begin to play!

Early in the Covid 19 pandemic, I sorted out several large boxes of Lego, that had belonged to our children, when they were growing up. With the help of the instructions, I slowly assembled all the kits that I was able to. What amazed me was finding the tiny specialist bricks, without which the kits would have been incomplete. They were still there; they just needed finding and positioning! This is what apostles do, to help teams come into being. They recognise the times and the seasons; when to move forward and when to stop. They also listen to God, and let Him show them which people to approach, to consider working with them as part of a team.

## MALE AND FEMALE PERSPECTIVES

Perspectives from the opposite sex can be very helpful in clarifying how apostles should form their teams.

Ideally, you should expect the teams that God gives, will have both men and women in them. Our God reflects both male and female attributes, and as He has made man, male and female - in His image; we would expect that, in most contexts, the teams of His choosing will have both males and females in them. That way the full counsel of God can be represented.

However, if the team does not contain men and women, we can still rejoice! In practice, God works with the people that are there on the ground and available. He can still give us insights, from both the male and female point of view, because He is not only the LORD of Hosts but also El Shaddai – the One who nourishes us at the breast. In any case, believers, men and women, are both sons of God (Gal.3:26-28), and the beloved bride of Christ (2 Cor.11:2). Therefore they are spiritually in a position to have insights from both male and female perspectives.

## A COMPANY OF WOMEN

In the context of both the regional, and the international, our current experience is that God has surrounded us with a company of women! Maybe that's your situation too? Mary and I are part of an international prophetic and apostolic grouping, and it has been a great learning curve to be involved on their teams, in various projects and events. Of course, there are some men involved, but the majority of the group are women.

We have felt the truth of the words, *'The LORD announced the word, and great was the company of those who proclaimed it'* (Ps.68:11). The Hebrew word for 'those who proclaimed it' is a feminine word! In this passage, an army of women are announcing the arrival of the God who saves (Ps.68:19-20). Similarly, the subject and verb in, *'You who bring good tidings to*

*Zion...'* (Isa 40:9) is feminine. This company of women, are seen as a great army, deployed and ready for battle.

## AN ARMY OF GRANDMOTHERS

One time, during this last year, Mary and I heard God speaking to us, through a photograph of an open book - we could make out just one word on the page – 'grandmother'! This struck us as being a word for apostles to emphasise, in this season. God wants to stir up the grandmothers to help the generations below them. The whole Malachi, chapter four passage comes to mind, about turning the hearts of the fathers to the sons, and the hearts of the sons to the fathers (Mal.4:6). Grandmothers are called to draw down blessings on their children and their children's children; but not just biologically! We believe that right now, younger people have an ache for 'grandmother' figures. This younger generation is craving stability, acceptance and love, and grandmothers can fill this gap in their lives. So, it is important for apostles to encourage the bringing in of the grandmothers. If you are a grandmother reading this, hear the permission that the Lord is giving you, to work inter-generationally. By all means, bless and care for your family, but be ready, also, to be a 'grandmother' to many others!

Interestingly, football clubs were having trouble with hooliganism in Brazil, and as they thought about what they could do, the idea of grandmothers came up, as a solution! They hired a whole crowd of grandmothers to stand between the rival fans at their events, and it worked a treat! Grandmothers were held in such regard that they worked far better than the police, or security stewards. Their presence really sorted the situation out, and brought peace. That is something for us to think about! We really feel spiritually that this is going to be the season for the grandmother. So get ready grandmothers!

# THE MIGHTY MEN WHO HELP US

The LORD surrounds us, not only with Himself, but with some 'mighty men' as a team, to encourage us. Through them, God can remind us of who He is, and how He sees us. These 'mighty men' may be male or female, either way they are there to help us.

## A TEAM COMES TOGETHER

We see in chapters eleven and twelve of First Chronicles, long lists of the 'mighty men' that gathered around David. God was raising up a team, to fulfill His plans and purposes for David, and the people of Israel. Some of them had come to join David when he was on the run and hiding in the Cave of Adulam; others joined him later, in Ziklag, when he was officially in league with the Philistines; still others, later joined him at Hebron, in the final period before he was anointed king over the whole of Israel.

## RAW MATERIALS

Those who came to join David at the cave of Adullam are not described in glowing terms. They didn't look much like a quality team.
*'All those who were in distress, or in debt, or discontented gathered around him and he became their leader'* (1 Sam.22:2).

The men who came to join David were men who did not fit in elsewhere. They had messed up, or were just really unhappy. However, these discontented ones had recognized that there had to be something more for them, out of life, than what seemed to be on offer. The messed up ones wanted to start again, and those in distress just wanted to be happy!

Like David, the team which the LORD gives for an apostle to work with, may not be all that one might wish! Nevertheless, it can have the momentum to change. God is well able to start with these raw materials and do a wonderful transforming work, from the most unpromising of beginnings!

## A QUALITY TEAM

We read later, in First Chronicles, about how David's team had got on. The final description of the 'mighty men' around him (1Ch.12:22-40), is a very encouraging one. An amazing fighting force had been brought together, entirely fitted to sweep David into power, even as the army of Israel, under King Saul, lay collapsed on the battlefield before the Philistines.

The 'mighty men' are described as armed for battle; ready and prepared, fighting men, or warriors, with every kind of weapon for attack and defence. They were brave, fully determined, of one mind, understanding the times, and knowing what should be done. They were experienced men, well-known for their undivided loyalty and faithfulness. They had come willingly, as volunteers prepared to serve – as leaders, or in the ranks; in whatever way David needed them. They were fully determined to fulfil God's plan to make David king (1 Ch.12:38). What a transformation!

Along with the 'mighty men' came quality 'gold-standard' support. Families and neighbours had brought food in plentiful supplies; and all the means for good transportation in the form of donkeys, camels, mules and oxen! The team and the provision had arrived (1 Ch.12:39-40)!

## MUTUAL HELP

God will bring apostles the team that they need around them; if they are willing for Him to do so. However, it is not only apostles who can expect God to give them a team. None of us are called to live in isolation from the rest of the Body of Christ. Therefore, every believer can expect God to give them some 'team' to help them. The question we need to ask ourselves is:-

*'Who has God put into my life as a 'mighty men' team, to help me fulfill everything He wants to do, through me?'*

Out there, perhaps not quite in the way we expected, or wished for, is our quality team!

However, there is also a similar question to ask in reverse:-

*'For whom, is God calling me to be a 'mighty man', in order to help them fulfill His purposes in their life?'*

It is time for us to follow the example of Jesus, and serve one another in whatever way is needed, and not just think of our own personal needs. As we give our lives in service, a wonderful promise comes into action, summarised by Jesus, in this way, *'Give and it will be given to you. A good measure, pressed down, shaken together and running over, will be poured into your lap. For with the measure you use, it will be measured to you'* (Lk.6:38).

## VISIONARY NAMES

Even when things were looking bleak for David, I believe that God was encouraging him by faith, through the names of the men who had come to join him. Their names had meanings. As each one came and gave his name, David would have been reminded, more than we might think, that the LORD was with him, and that God was big enough to help him. For example, when someone says, 'Hi, my name is Eliphal', it takes on a whole new level of encouragement, when one realises it means, *'Miracle of God'* (1 Ch.11:35). How good is that!

So looking at just the first ten names of these mighty men whom the LORD brought to support David, we can see how encouraged he would have been, not just by the men themselves, but also by the names they were carrying.

From the first ten, we have:-
*'God is the One who fashions us, who makes us who we are'* (Asahel),
*'He is the One who graciously gives'* (Elhanan),
*'the LORD is our strength'* (Helez),
*'the One who is attentive and watchful over us'* (Ira),
*'the Father of our support and help'* (Abiezer),
*'the LORD who sustains us'* (Sibbecai),
*'the One who is exalted'* (Ilai),
*'the One who sees the whole of life, the big picture'* (Heled), and
*'He is not tardy but swift on our behalf'* (Maharai) (1 Ch.11:26-30).

These are truths about which the LORD wanted to remind David. God will also bring a 'mighty men' team into our lives, to remind us about the truths of who He is. It may not be through the meaning of their names, but God will be encouraging us, in a similar way to David, to walk by faith, and listen to what our team might be saying to us, about Him.

I believe God also wanted to encourage David through the names of these 'mighty men', in a different way.

He wanted him to believe that he too could emulate the LORD by being:-
gracious like Elhanan,
strong like Helez,
watchful like Ira,
helpful and supportive like Abiezer,
seeing the bigger picture like Heled, and being
swift and quick when it was needed like Maharai,
and (one other name, not yet mentioned of these first ten)
thirsty for God like Shammoth.

The full list of all the 'mighty men' listed in this passage from First Chronicles, with the meanings of their names, is in an appendix for you to think more about later (see page 199).
As an exercise, why not see which ones particularly encourage you, from the meaning of their names. Perhaps, the team that God gives you, will especially carry those qualities.

When we meet someone, we sometimes see the way which a person may be used in our lives. Jesus saw Simon, and called him Peter – the rock. He saw James and John and called them Sons of Thunder. The first apostles gave a man named Joseph, the name Barnabas, which means Son of Encouragement (Acts 4:36).

In prayer, we may like to ask God to show us the roles others might have in our life, and the roles we might have in theirs. He has fitted together His team, and wants us to find our proper place in it. We need to understand the 'name' we might be for the team.

**What name might you be called, by someone who appreciates you being part of *their* team?**

## WOVEN TOGETHER

Together, Mary and I sense that a robust, yet delicate, work is being done, through the teams God has raised up in our area. We hope you sense the same in the area where you live. We sense that the teams in our area have been *'woven together in the fabric of God's love'* (Col.2:2), and have become companions with us, in the work of God. A spiritual patchwork is being sewn together; as everyone shares their anointing within their particular teams. Mary and I have teams for most of the things we do. Whether it is for planning a prayer day, or starting a gospel choir, God will give us a team.

Our teams are very flexible. We feel that together, God is making us like a piece of strong, but delicate, silk, which can slip through small places, and yet cover a large area. The name of each one of us has been woven uniquely into the cloth, and together we have become the train of His glory, spread out over our region!

## PARTNERSHIPS

Apostles will always be looking for others with whom they can align themselves, in partnership. Their purpose isn't to create hierarchical structures, but relational networks, which will bring revival to a region, or a nation.

We need wisdom to navigate the structures through which the church currently operates; and wisdom to build 'platforms of agreement' with others, in order to bring teams together with common goals. The role of an apostle is that of a diplomat! Wise apostles will create forums, which will encourage partnerships and connections. They do this by providing opportunities to unpack and discuss helpful input; by sharing experiences and collective wisdom; by hearing about imaginative and creative mission ideas, and by praying for one another.

## NEW THINGS

New ways of being church are emerging at this present time. There is experimentation going on, in structures, approaches, job roles and the language used to describe these things. God has been suppressing the old to allow the new to emerge. There are strands being picked up, ready for the new. It is time to weave them together into new patterns, while still continuing to give honour to those things already in place. A good understanding and willingness to be part of a team, serving others and also being served, is essential for the new 'churches' to come into being.

**Placed in the train of His glory**

# PART FOUR
# PRESENTING

How apostles help us to get ready for the final outcome, when we are presented as a beautiful, holy Bride of Christ, in a deep communion of relationships with God and one another.

# Alphabet of Love

An Acrostic poem (each line/idea starts with a letter in the sequence of the Alphabet). This is a Love poem from the Bridegroom (Jesus) to His Bride (the Church).

Awake, arise, My awesome one, the apple of My eye,

Believe you belong to Me, beautiful you are!

Cuddle close to Me, let Me comfort and caress,

Drink deeply of My love, darling, draw nearer

Enter My embrace!

Feel free to follow My example,

Gaze upon my face,

And in the gazing, may there be a giving

Holding hands in happiness.

Invite Me into your ideas, imagine and inspire;

Join with Me on a journey to joy,

That will never, ever tire!

Kiss Me, O kiss Me quickly

Love Me long and deep;

Melt My heart a million times

Nuzzle nearer, and never leave!

Overwhelmed, I observe you, over and over again;
Passionately you pursue Me,
Quivering with delight, yet queenly in your frame,
Run with Me, run with Me, My regal one
Surrender, I summon you; speaking out your name!

Tell Me the truth about the two of us,
A tale deserves to be told,
Understand I will love you always
Even when you are old!

Vanquished, My heart is conquered,
As, unveiled, My bride appears,
Walking in white towards Me,
While I wipe away My tears.

Ecstatic in My excitement,
I extend My hand and heart,
Yearning to be united, My beloved,
Zipped together; never more to part!

Mary Bain  September 2018

# CHAPTER FIFTEEN
## PRESENTING THE BRIDE

*The church can be understood as the bride of Christ, getting herself ready for her wedding day. Apostles help her in her preparations.*

*The New Jerusalem - Making herself ready - The father of the bride - A mystery - The work of the Trinity - The Ascension gifts - Paul the match-maker - Esther's beauty preparations - The royal bride - Treasure in jars of clay – Tamar, restoring order*

## THE NEW JERUSALEM

'*Let us rejoice and be glad and give Him glory! For the wedding of the Lamb has come, and His bride has made herself ready*' (Rev.19:7). There is a future wedding date, to which we are all looking forward, described in the final chapters of the Bible. The church is coming to her own wedding; she is invited to '*the wedding supper of the Lamb*' (Rev.19:9).

She is described as a holy city, the New Jerusalem – '*coming down out of heaven from God, prepared as a bride beautifully dressed for her husband*' (Rev.21:2). When imagining the holy city, we shouldn't think so much about buildings, but rather what this city actually is – a network of relationships. The Bride has become a new creation of people, united together as one, in a godly network of relationships; and founded on the twelve apostles of the Lamb (Rev.21:14). She is the body of Christ, an intimately connected whole, of which every believer is a part (1 Cor.12:27).

## MAKING HERSELF READY

Right now, the church is making herself ready, for the big day. As John says about the children of God, '*what we will be has not yet been made known. But we know that when He appears, we shall be like Him'* (1 Jn.3:2). This is her hope stirring up within her a desire to be holy. As John goes on to say, *'Everyone who has this hope in him purifies himself, just as He (Jesus) is pure'* (1 Jn.3:3).

When the day comes, the church will be ready. Paul wrote that the Lord Jesus *'will transform our lowly bodies so that they will be like his glorious body'* (Phil.3:21). We also have the assurance from John's vision in Revelation that the Bride will be presented, ready, on her wedding day, and beautifully dressed with fine linen - *'Fine linen, bright and clean, was given her to wear (Fine linen stands for the righteous acts of the saints)'* (Rev.19:8). We have no need to panic – it will be alright on the day! The church is making herself ready; but she is also getting a lot of help along the way.

## THE FATHER OF THE BRIDE

The church is not alone in her endeavour. Just like in the beginning of creation, when God presented the woman to the first man in the garden of Eden to be his wife, this is what the Father is now doing for His Son. He is at work, bringing forth a wonderful Bride for His Son, the Bridegroom. We have referred earlier in this book to God's relationship with His church, as being a parenting one. God's aim, as Father, was always to bring the church to full maturity, in order to present her to His Son, as a perfect bride. Our growth into maturity as Christians has had a purpose!

This is the amazing master plan, that the church might be joined forever, in union with her husband, Jesus – to become one body with him, *'for we are members of His body'* (Eph.5:30). In this same passage, Paul goes on to quote Genesis, *'For this reason a man will leave his father and mother and be united to his wife, and the two will become one flesh'* (Eph 5:31). Jesus and His church have become one.

# A MYSTERY

Paul calls this plan *'a profound mystery'*, stressing that he is talking about Christ and the church (Eph.5:32). The Greek word, translated *'mystery'*, means something that was hidden, which is then suddenly revealed. This is the mystery that Paul says was made known to him by revelation, *'the mystery of Christ, which was not made known to men in other generations as it has now been revealed by the Spirit to God's holy apostles and prophets'* (Eph.3:3-5).

John, also got to see the great reveal of this mystery when he saw, in a vision, the Bride of Christ on her wedding day coming down from heaven (Rev.21:2).

## THE WORK OF THE TRINITY

Not just the Father, but the whole Trinity has been involved in helping the church get ready. The final work has been a united one, displayed in the whole church, to the glory of God. *'Now to Him who is able to do immeasurably more than all we ask or imagine, according to His power that is at work within us, to Him be glory in the church and in Christ Jesus throughout all generations, for ever and ever! Amen'* (Eph.3:20-21).

It has been the full-on work of the undivided Trinity of God! They have all been engaged in the process, Father, Son and Holy Spirit.

Jesus, as the bridegroom, is at work presenting her *'to himself as a radiant church'* (Eph.5:27). He has wooed her in a courtship described in chapter after chapter of Song of Songs, pouring out words of love and invitation over her. He invited her to come away with him, *'My lover spoke and said to me, Arise, my darling, my beautiful one, and come with me'* (SS.2:10). He came to the earth to rescue her, and to bring her to be with himself forever. He has laid down his life for his bride, *'Christ loved the church and gave Himself up for her'* (Eph.5:25).

In this time of wedding preparation, the Spirit has been given to her as a Helper, to make her ready, by producing good fruit within her (Gal.5:22-23). The Spirit hovered over the church, and gave each of us new birth, as children of God in the first place, just as He hovered over the waters at the start of creation. The Spirit is also her engagement ring, with which she has been sealed, a deposit within her, guaranteeing what is to come (Eph.1:13-14). He has also been busy interceding for the saints, in accordance with God's will, while they have waited eagerly for what is to come (Rom.8:23 -26). The Spirit, along with the Bride is saying, *'Come'* (Rev.22:17).

The Father parented her, the Son gave Himself up for her and the Spirit has helped her. The church is in the centre of this divine process. She cries out, with the Spirit, to her Father God, *'Abba, Father'* (Gal.4:6), and to Jesus, her Bridegroom, she calls out, *'Come'*.

## THE ASCENSION GIFTS

The five Ascension gifts are also working with the Bride, to get her ready for her wedding day. As we have seen earlier, in the Parenting section of this book, God the Father has highlighted them in His parenting process - the apostles, prophets, evangelists, pastors and teachers. They are all there in the wedding preparations, and working under His direction _with_ the bride. There has been a wonderful, joyful reason why they were needed to help the church to become mature. Paul, for example, wrote to the Corinthians that he was working _with them,_ for their joy (2 Cor.1:24). The apostles, prophets, evangelists, pastors and teachers stand apart from the church for a moment, and fuss around her, tidying up this and that bit of the dress, while she stands in front of the mirror of the Word of God!

Each Ascension gift applies their different gifting, and the bride is presented as a radiant beauty, *'without stain or wrinkle or any other blemish but holy and blameless'* (Eph.5:27). This is the process in which the five-fold gifts are engaged. It is a vision that we should all get excited about!

## PAUL THE MATCH-MAKER

Paul describes the Corinthian believers in these terms – *'I promised you to one husband, to Christ, so that I might present you as a pure virgin to him'* (2 Cor.11:2). The King James version translates it this way, *'I espoused you'*, the Revised Standard version, *'I betrothed you'*. The different versions are all having a go at translating the Greek word, *'harmozo'*, which means, *'to fit'*, or *'to join'*.

Paul has been busy bringing the church up to a point of readiness, to be joined to her future spouse. His aim was to present her; literally *'place her alongside'* Christ, as His bride. Paul frames his role then, as that of a match-maker, or even as the father of the bride; ensuring that the bride will indeed be presented as a pure virgin, on her wedding day. To the Colossians, Paul wrote that he had been working hard in order to present them all perfect (Col.1:28). Paul told the Corinthians that everything he did was for their strengthening (2 Cor.12:19), and that his prayer was for their perfection (2 Cor.13:9). We can see that Paul, as an apostle, was busy preparing the bride.

## ESTHER'S BEAUTY PREPARATIONS

A wedding day is coming for the church, and a beautifying process has been going on. Like Esther, we are being made ready for our presentation before the King. In Esther's case, she was given special food and twelve months of beauty treatments under the care of Hegai, with seven maids in attendance (Es.1:8-12). He was there to watch over her, and to make her ready.

Hegai's name means, *separation, groaning, meditation*, or just simply, *word*. For people with an interest in the meaning of names, there is always a danger of pressing meanings into names, to make them foreshadow some aspect of the salvation story. So you are welcome to make your own conclusions, but certainly, Hegai's work, like Paul the apostle's, was to keep his charge *separate* from other distractions, and to engage her in a continual and exacting process of preparation, ahead of the day of her presentation. Meditation and groaning would suggest the kind of process both Hegai, and Paul, went through, (not to mention, Esther!); perhaps indicative of teaching on how to receive God's word and praying in the Spirit.

## THE ROYAL BRIDE

Psalm forty-five provides an awesome description of a royal bride, as she is presented before the king, on her wedding day (Ps.45:10-17). *'All glorious is the princess within her chamber; her gown is interwoven with gold. In embroidered garments she is led to the king'* (Ps.45:13-14). It is a wonderful foreshadowing of Christ and His church. The author of Hebrews quotes this Psalm as being about the Son of God (Heb.1:8-9), so it is not fanciful to see the royal bride as a foreshadowing of the church. In the psalm, the bride is told to listen up and consider this instruction – *'Forget your people and your father's house'* (Ps.45:10). She was to forget the past, and press forward to the goal set before her. She is told to *'honour [the king] for he is your Lord'* (Ps.45:11).

## TREASURE IN JARS OF CLAY

For Paul, the vision of the church as the royal bride of Christ, will have encouraged him to keep going in his task. The people with whom he worked, outwardly, looked nothing like a glorious bride! When he looked at the newly formed Corinthian church, for example, he saw a motley group, not wise, not influential, not of noble birth. God had truly chosen the foolish and weak things of this world (1 Cor.1:26-27). They had been sexually immoral, idolaters, adulterers, male prostitutes, homosexual offenders, thieves, greedy, drunkards, slanderers and swindlers (1 Cor.6:10-11). These were the raw materials with which Paul the apostle was being called to work. The bride did not come ready-made! No wonder Paul said that he walked by faith, not by sight (2 Cor.5:7). But he had confidence that there was treasure in those jars of clay, and that the power, at work in them, was of God not of themselves.

*'But we have this treasure in jars of clay to show that this all-surpassing power is from God and not from us'* (2 Cor.4:7).

-------------------------------------------------------------------------

# CONCLUSION
# TAMAR – RESTORING ORDER

The bride has a problem in getting herself ready – the apostles, prophets, evangelists, pastors and teachers are in confusion and a muddle. There is a need to restore some proper order and understanding of their roles. At the moment, they are often operating in an environment, uncooperative and hostile to their proper functioning.

I feel Tamar provides a good illustration of the experiences that the five-fold gifts can face. You can read Tamar's story in Genesis chapter thirty-eight. Through her persistence, she secured her future; in spite of the mess in which she found herself. Tamar goes on a journey of faith with the people of God. Like the widow before the unjust judge, through persistence, she obtained a good outcome in the end (Luke 18:1-8). Proper order was finally restored, and there was blessing, and Tamar's baby became part of the family tree of Jesus. She found favour with God, and He included her in her proper place in the household of faith.

Like Tamar, the five-fold gifts didn't get to choose their circumstances. They are having to function in the church, in the state in which it exists, however messy and hostile the environment might be. In Tamar's story, her future was being shut down. She was supposed to be getting married, but instead she was left in limbo. Similarly, the five-fold gifts can be shut out, shut down, or simply left in limbo in the church. They can be shut in, and told to shut up! But in spite of the opposition, they have the favour of God on them, and He has determined to include them, and position them, like Tamar, in their proper place in the household of faith.

In the words of Paul, '*And in the church God has appointed first of all, **apostles**, second **prophets**, third **teachers**...*' (1 Cor.12:28).

The wedding preparations for presenting the Bride of Christ to her husband, will be made considerably more straight-forward, when we recognise those whom God has appointed, and give them room to function in their correct order.

# APPENDIX I
## DAVID'S MIGHTY MEN
## 1 Chronicles chapters 11 and 12

Here is the full list of names from this passage with meanings taken from various google-searched references.

**1 Chron. Chap.11**
**Jashobeam** v11 Let the people return, Let the people be released, He will return among the people
**Eleazar,** v12 God has helped
**Abishai,** v20 Father of a gift
**Benaiah,** v.22 Son of the LORD, built up of the LORD
**Asahel** v26 made by God, fashioned by God
**Elhanan** v26 God is good, God is gracious
**Shammoth** v27 thirsty
**Helez** v27 strong
**Ira** v28 watchful, attentive, roused
**Abiezer** v28 Father of help, support

**Sibbecai** v29 The LORD sustains
**Ilai** v29 exalted, high
**Mahari** v30 quick, swift
**Heled** v30 life, duration – the whole scene, the big picture
**Ithai** v31 strong, a ploughshare
**Benaiah** v31 Son of the LORD, built up of the LORD
**Hurai** v32 Free, noble
**Abiel** v32 God is my Father
**Azmaveth** v33 strong to death
**Eliahba** v33 God conceals, hides

**Jonathan** v34 God has given
**Ahiam** v35 friend of the mother(land)
**Eliphal** v35 A miracle of God

**Hepher** v36  well, pit or shame
**Ahijah** v36 brother of the LORD
**Hezro** v37  the arrow of joy
**Naarai** v37  a child of the LORD
**Joel** v38  The LORD is God
**Mibhar** v38 the best, selected by preference
**Zelek** v39 loyal, unwavering

**Naharai** v39 to snort hotly, sudden explosive sounds!
**Ira** v40  watchful, attentive, roused
**Gareb** v40  scab, a hardened protection
**Uriah** v41  light of the LORD, the flame of God
**Zabad** v41 endowed, a gift
**Adina** v42  pleasant, luxury, delight
**Hanan** v43  gracious, merciful
**Joshaphat** v43  the LORD rules, the LORD governs
**Uzzia** v44  The LORD is my Strength, the LORD is strong
**Shama**  v44  obedient, listens, hears

**Jiel** v44  the LORD is God
**Jediael** v45  the knowledge of God, known of God
**Joha** v45  enlivens, gives life
**Eliel** v46  My God is God
**Jeribai** The LORD contends
**Joshaviah** v46  The LORD supports, assists
**Ithmah** the one who needs a father, an orphan
**Eliel** v47  My God is God
**Obed** v47 servant of God
**Jaasiel** v47 God works, God does it, God makes it

**1 Chron. Chap.12**
**Ahiezer** 12:3  a brother who helps
**Joash** given by the LORD
**Jeziel** God sprinkled, assembled by God
**Pelet** escape, deliverance

**Beracah** Blessing
**Jehu** The LORD is He, He is LORD
**Ishmaiah** 12:4 hearing , obeying the LORD, the LORD hears
**Jeremiah** raised up, appointed by the LORD
**Jahaziel** God sees, God looks
**Johanan** The LORD is gracious

**Jozabad** Endowed by the LORD, the LORD has given
**Eluzai** 12:5 God is my strength, my refuge
**Jerimoth** Rain of death, elevation, high places, to reject death
**Bealiah** The LORD is lord, is master
**Shemariah** The LORD is my guard, my keeper,
**Shephatiah** The LORD judges, governs
**Elkanah** 12:6 God has acquired, God-created
**Isshiah** Salvation of the LORD,
**Azarel** God has helped, God is the helper
**Joezer** The LORD is our help

**Jashobeam** Let the people return, Let the people be released,
He will return among the people
**Joelah** 12:7 lifting up, taking away slander, profiting
**Zebadiah** The LORD has bestowed, Gift of the LORD
**Ezer** 12:9 Help
**Obadiah** servant of the LORD
**Eliab** My God is Father
**Mishmannah** 12:10 Fatness, abundance to overflowing
**Jeremiah** raised up, appointed by the LORD
**Attai** 12:11 timely, opportune
**Eliel** My God is God

**Johanan** 12:12 The LORD is gracious
**Elzabad** God has given
**Jeremiah** 12:13 raised up, appointed by the LORD
**Macbannai** hilly, a hill
**Amasai** The LORD has carried, the burden of the LORD

**Adnah** 12:20  Delightful brother
**Jozabad**  Endowed by the LORD, the LORD has given
**Jediael**  the knowledge of God, known of God
**Michael**  Gift from God, who is like God ?
**Jozabad**  Endowed by the LORD, the LORD has given

**Elihu**  My God is He, My God is the LORD
**Zillethai**  The shadow of the LORD, the bell of the LORD, the LORD rings
**Jehoiada** 12:26  The LORD knows
**Zadok** 12:28  righteous, justified

# APPENDIX II
# APOSTLES – THE BASICS

**APOSTLES** are an important building block, helping to equip the church.

## A.  SENT

**THE BASIC DEFINITION** of the Greek word, *'apostolos'*, translated, apostle, means simply, *'a sent one'*.
**If you have been sent by someone, with their authority to do something, as if they themselves were present, then you are their apostle.**

**SENT BY CHRIST.** Apostles are particularly **sent by Christ**, called and sent on assignment by the will of God. The sense of being sent by God's will, ('sentness'), describes the foundational influence they have towards us. Through the influence of apostles, we discover, that we are all on assignment. As 'sent ones', apostles impart an aroma of 'sentness' to the church – a scent of 'sentness'.

**POWER AND DEPENDENCY.** Apostles are entirely **dependent on God** in everything - power on the one hand and vulnerability on the other; sent with an authority based on their relationship with God.

They come in ordinary human packaging, both men and women. Apostles will encounter **opposition**, but with it, God promises that He will make a way through it all.

**CALLING AND TERRITORY.** Apostles have a call to work in specific areas or regions, governing the territory with worship, prophetic singing, and prayer walking

# B.   PARENTING

**The aim** of our Father God is that *'the body of Christ may be built up… and become mature, attaining to the whole measure of the fulness of Christ'* (Eph.4:12).

Paul shares **God's heart** in fatherly and motherly terms in 1 Thess.2:7, 11-12. He shows us the nature of God as a parent, as he describes his own relationship as an apostle in the church.

**ASCENSION GIFTS.** 'It was he [the Christ] who gave some to be apostles, some to be prophets, some to be evangelists, and some to be pastors and teachers… (Eph.4:11).
Together in God's parenting process, the Ascension gifts bring about a wonderful maturing of the body of Christ, as God graciously gives, through them, all we need to be equipped for our particular 'work of service' (Eph.4:12-13).

**PARENTS.** God's parenting process is being **modelled by parents** when they function as apostles, prophets, evangelists, pastors and teachers. In particular, **parents**, **as apostles**, do the following:-
**Purpose and calling.** Parents help establish a sense of purpose and calling in their children's lives
**The adventure of discovery.** Parents take their children on an exciting adventure of discovery of the world around them, and their place in it - a person's process of discovery and formation of themselves. They introduce them to new experiences in which they find out more about themselves and their identity.
**Establishing.** Parents are not only there to help their children understand their purpose in life, but also to help establish them in it. They encourage and support their children to keep going, to enjoy who they are, and what God has called them to be.

**Overview.** Parents need to give their children overview to help them stay true to God's plan. Parents are on the look out to connect their children with opportunities which are in line with God's plan. From time to time, their children's attitudes may need challenging and disturbing.

# C.  BUILDING

Apostles establish God's purposes on the earth. They initiate the moving of God's people back into their proper position. They are builders – they initiate and implement the new things that God is doing. They lay the foundations. They get the plumb line out, and check that the walls are being built true and straight.

The foundations of the church are the apostles and prophets with Christ as the chief cornerstone (Eph.2:20). Just like the foundations of a building, apostles are undergirding and supporting everything going on in and through the church.

## HIDDEN QUALITIES.

**Hidden in the ordinary.** When Paul tells the church at Corinth to imitate his way of life, he wants them to follow the example of his ordinary, everyday life (1 Cor.4:16-17).

**The apostle's hidden place of intimacy with God** is having a profound effect on what we can see outwardly.

**There is a bigger story, hidden from sight, foundational experiences** that apostles need to communicate - key moments that will be of benefit to others.

**They have a hidden influence on people** - like mother and father figures. Their teaching continues to influence in the background.

**COMMUNICATIONS** are at the heart of the work of apostles; they are essential communicators in helping the church grow. Apostles spend a lot of time bringing people together and making connections. **Through this they are building relationships.**

**Connections need to be maintained.** A constant stream of communication is needed, initiated by apostles - **news, reports and evidence, communicating arrangements, travel help, and letters of recommendation,** (apostles provide reassurance that visiting believers can be trusted).

## ENCOURAGEMENT

**Apostles may 'pop-up' unpredictably** - in places and people's lives, and with them come God's words of encouragement. They have authority from God to build up and not to tear down (2 Cor.10:8).

**People are encouraged** by apostles sharing their experience, and giving practical help on how to go forward. Blockages may occur because people don't know how to move on. Apostles can act as sounding boards to help people begin again. They help them navigate to where they wanted to go. They bring breakthrough, releasing people caught up in the darkness and grip of the enemy. They release a different spiritual atmosphere in an area. Their activities can re-set the culture.
**The influence of apostles wakes us up;** and we become aware of, and released into, our calling and purpose in God.
**Apostles remind us of who we are in Christ,** and the noble task, in which we are engaged.

**Apostles stir up a mutual giving and receiving of support and encouragement** between believers, stirring up the churches to support one another, and also to pray and give support to those elsewhere.

## OVERVIEW

**Apostles bring overview and strategy.** Their understanding of the bigger picture of God's plans and purposes helps people to see what they are doing in the details of their lives, with a new perspective.

**Identifying and resourcing.** Apostles identify the spiritual and other needs of our communities. They also reveal the strengths and weaknesses in how the church, as a whole, is functioning, and establish relevant ministry projects. In a changing environment, apostles help us to re-imagine the possibilities of what might be ahead.

## APOSTLES DISTURB.

They disturb old paradigms. They go in and break things up that have lost their relevancy. They help to break down bad thinking and encourage good thinking.

## TEAMS AND PARTNERSHIPS.

Apostles help get teams started. They look for others with whom they can partner. They want to create relational networks, which will bring revival to a region, or a nation.

# D.   PRESENTING

The five Ascension gifts are working with the bride to get her ready for her wedding day. They work, under God's direction, with the bride, helping her to become mature. Apostles understand their role, as that of a match-maker, or even as the father of the bride, ensuring that the bride will indeed be presented as a pure virgin on her wedding day.

# STUDY OUTLINE
## SENTNESS
## HOW APOSTLES HELP US TO BE APOSTOLIC

*'A green shoot will come up from the stump of Jesse; from his roots a Branch will bear fruit'* (Isa.11:1).

## PART ONE - SENT

How apostles help us to understand our sense of purpose – the way we are positioned and handle power in dependency, our vulnerability and relationship with God, and our calling and areas of operation.

## CHAPTER ONE - 'SENTNESS'

This word 'sentness' that we have coined in the title of this book, seems to aptly describe the primary characteristic, which we believe apostles impart to the church. They give us a sense of purpose and direction.

Gifts from on high  Eph.4:8, 11
First of all, apostles  1 Cor.12:28, Eph.2:20
Umbrella anointing  1 Cor.12:7
An atmosphere of influence
The influence of the first apostles
No super-apostles  2 Cor.11:1-15
Ordinary packaging
The basic definition  Phil.2:25
An apostle of Christ  Gal.1:1, Acts 13:1-3, , Acts 14:4
Sent by the will of God  1 Cor.1:1
An aroma of sentness

## CHAPTER TWO - POWER AND DEPENDENCY

Apostles are sent out in power <u>and</u> dependency. If we look at the detail of how Jesus sent out the Twelve and then later, the

Seventy-two, we see how he wanted the apostles to always recognise their dependency on him. This lesson is summarised in Jesus words, 'apart from me you can do nothing' (Jn.15:5) - we are entirely dependent on him in everything.

A lesson for the twelve Jn.15:5, Mk.3:14-15, Mk.6:13, Lk.9:52,
Mk.6:31

A lesson over a meal
A lesson in a boat Mk.6:45, Mk.6:48, Jn.6:21, Mk.6:48,
Mt.14:29-30

The seventy-two Lk.10:17, Lk.10:20
Little children  Lk.10:21, Lk.10:22
Little flock  Lk.12:11, Lk.12:32, Jn.10:11, 14
Sent in powerful vulnerability  Mt.10:7-8
A herd of bulls Lk.10:18-19, Mt.11:12, Josh.1:9
Lambs among wolves  Mt.10:16, Lk.10:3, Mt. 9:36, Mt.10:6
Reliance on others  Mt.10:9-10, Lk.10:5-7, Mt.10:42
Received or rejected  Lk.10:16
Yoked oxen  Mt.10:24-25, Lk.6:40, Mt.11:29
Meek nobility  Prov.14:4
Washing feet  Mt.20:28, Jn.13:13-16, Mk.10:44, Mt.20:25-26

## CHAPTER THREE - AUTHORITY AND RELATIONSHIP

Apostles are sent with authority, but what in practice does this mean?  There is a lesson for us to learn, that we are all sent with authority; and our exercise of it grows, as our relationship with God grows.

The authority of Jesus  Mt.28:18, Heb.3:1
A growing understanding  Lk.2:46-47, Jn. 5:19, Jn.3:34, Jn.8:28,
Jn.4:34, Jn.17:22, Jn.14:9

An intimate relationship
The authority of the apostles Jn.17:18, Jn.20:21, Jn.13:16,
Friendship with Jesus  Mk.3:14-15, Jn.15:15

The presence of the Spirit  Acts 4:13, Jn.14:17, Jn.16:13-15,
Jn.16:7, Jn.14:16
The extension of the mission  Jn.17:22, Jn.17:20-21, Jn.17:21
Signs and wonders, John 4:35, 2 Cor.6:2, Mt.10:7-8, Lk.10:9,
2 Cor.12:12, Rom.15:18-19, Mk.16:18

## CHAPTER FOUR - NEEDED
Apostles find us and release us into the harvest field. They tell
us that we, too, are needed.
1 Cor.12:21, 2 Cor.6:1, 2 Cor.5:20, 1Tim 2:3-4


Donkeys on a big mission
Found and released  Mt.21:1-2
Responding to opposition  Lk.19:33 , Mk.11:5-6, Mt.21:3,
Eph.4:16
Reminded of our mission  Mt.20:6, Mt.20:7

## CHAPTER FIVE - CALLING
There is a way chosen for us by God in which He promises to
guide us (Ps.25:12). Our lives truly are in His hands – He has
called us, and fashioned us, for things only we can do. There
are '…good works which God prepared in advance for us to
do' (Eph.2:10). No-one can change God's calling on their lives.
God is the one who calls, and He is at the beginning and at the
end of the process, and all the way through the middle as
well.
Ps.25:12, Eph.2:10, Ps.139:16


'Not me, lord!'  Ex.4:1, Ex.4:10, Ex.4:12, Ex.4:13
Something more  Gal.5:25
'I am has sent me' Ex.3:14 , 1 Cor.15:10
A Cyrus mission
God's appointment  2 Ch.36:23, Isa.44:28, Isa.45:1, Isa.45:3,
Isa.46:13, Ps.139:13-16
Declaring the move

Rebuilding  Isa.44:26 , Isa.44:28, Isa.46:13, 1 Cor.3:10
Subduing opposition  Isa.45:1-2, 1 Cor.16:7, Ro.8:35, 37
Breaking through barriers  Isa 45:1-2,  Ps 107:16
Given hidden treasures  Isa.45:3 Heb.12:2, Heb.2:13, Mt.13:44
Finding direction, Ps.27:4, Acts 13:1-3

## CHAPTER SIX - TERRITORY

God gives specific assignments to each one of us, in the places where He has sent us. There is a general sense of calling, but then there is the detail of our positioning. Apostles remind us, that we are where we are for a reason. We may think we live in a place because of our job, or to be near the grandchildren, or because we were born there, but in fact, God has positioned us there. Acts 17:26

Sent to the ends of the earth
No limits
Paul's sense of territory  Gal.2:7-8, 2 Cor.10:13, 2 Cor.10:15-16
The work done by others  2 Cor.10:16, 1 Cor.3:5-6, Rom.15:23,
                                                              Rom.15:24
New territory in the north
A bigger shift than expected
The God who opens doors  Rom.15:20, Rev.3:7-8, Isa.45:1,
                                                              Eph.2:10
Governorship  Isa.22:15-25
Paul's Governorship  Col.1:25, 1 Cor.9:17, Eph.3:2, 1 Cor.16:9,
                                                              Col.4:3, Mt.7:7
Governing the territory with worship  Rom.12:1, Ps.8:2
Prophetic singing  Lk.4:18-19
Prayer walking the territory  Neh.3, Josh.1:3

## PART TWO - PARENTING
How apostles help us to grow up and mature as 'parents' ourselves with Father's love for those around us.

## CHAPTER SEVEN - THE PARENTING OF GOD
God is in the parenting business. This is the great enterprise that apostles, and all of us, are engaged in, and we need to understand what it might look like.

God our Father  Mt.6:9-13, Jn.1:12-13
A parenting passage  Eph.3:14 to 4:16
The parenting aim  Eph.4:12
To be like Jesus  2 Cor.3:18, 1 Jn.3:2
Becoming an adult  1 Thess.2:7, 1Thess.2:11-12
Fruitful discipline  Heb.12:10, Heb.12:11, Gal.5:22-23
Reproduction
Disciples making disciples  Mt.28:19-20
'In the name'
God's Gifts have purpose  Jn.14:16, 1 Cor.12:7, 11, Eph.4:15
The Ascension gifts  Eph.4:11
Hidden labels
Recognition after death
'One-size-fits-all pastors'
No lost generation
Missing labels
A faithful father  Ps.27:10, Eph.4:6
Equipped for the work of service  Eph.4:12-13
Our early experiences of apostles

## CHAPTER EIGHT - THE FIVE-FOLD GIFTED PARENT
Comparisons can be made between the Ascension gifts and good parents. Since they are part of God's parenting process, apostles should be amazing father figures, but we don't want to fall into the trap of thinking they are the only ones. We are going to look at how apostles fit in alongside the other four

gifts, by looking at how parents raise their children.

Parents reflect his image Mt.7:11, Lk.11:13

Parents as teachers
       Practical instruction  Prov.3:1-2
       Awesome wonder  Job chapters 38 to 41, Job 38:31-32,
                         Job 39 , Job 38:26-27, Col.3:16
       Expressing emotions Ps.42:5
       The word in every season  Psalm 119
Parents as pastors
       Intimacy Jn.10:14-15
       Protection  Jn.10:11, Mt.23:37, 1 Thess.2:7-8
       Feed my lambs  Jn.21:15-17
       Correction  2 Tim.3:16-17
       A Framework of Discipline
Parents as evangelists
       Town-crier moments  Acts 4:12, Josh.24:14-15
       Daily engagement
       Signs and wonders  Acts 8:6-7
Parents as prophets  1 Cor.14:3
       Recognising God's words  1 Sam 3:10
       Words to treasure  Lk.2:19, 49, 51
       Prophetic names
       Prophetic songs
       Bookmarks
Parents as apostles
       Purpose and calling
       The adventure of discovery
       Establishing
       Overview
Conclusion - God wants us all to be 'parents'
A growing self awareness  Eph.3:19
God is able  Eph.3:14-15, Eph.3:16-19, Eph.3:20, 2 Cor.4:16

## PART THREE - BUILDING

How apostles help us to relate and build one another up in our normal, ordinary lives – connecting, communicating, encouraging and supporting, disturbing and disrupting, and working with others as a team.

## CHAPTER NINE - HIDDEN AND UNPREDICTABLE

There is a hidden quality about much of the building work of apostles. More is going on than we may realise at first, in the way in which they are helping us. This is a different kind of work to that with bricks and mortar.

Underground animals  Prov.6:6, Mt.6:2
Hidden in the ordinary  1 Cor.4:16, Lk.17:10
More under the surface  2 Cor.12:2-4, Col.1:9, 1 Cor.14:18
A bigger story  2 Cor.11:24-27
Leadership is influence  1 Cor.1:12
Mother and father figures  1 Cor.4:14, 2 Cor.6:13, 1 Cor.4:15,
                                              Gal.4:19, 1 Thess.2:7, 11
Teaching  Mt.16:11-12, Mt.13:33, 2 Cor.3:2
Hidden foundations  Eph.2:20, 1 Cor.4:9
Unpredictable  Jn.3:8, Rom.8:14, Gal.5:16
Led to Macedonia  Acts 16:6-7
Led to Philippi  Acts.16:13-15

## CHAPTER TEN –
## COMMUNICATIONS AND CONNECTIONS

Apostles spend a lot of time bringing people together and making connections. Communications are at the heart of the work of an apostle, they are not an afterthought. The health of the church depends on them. They are essential in helping it grow.

Rabbits
Communicating foundational experiences  Acts 1:21-22
Apostles as communicators

Letters
Maintaining connections  3 Jn.13-14 , 1 Thess.3:1-5, 1 Thess.3:6,
1 Thess.5:27
The human connection
Greetings  Col.1:2, Col.4:14, Rom.16:3-16
News  2 Cor.1:15 - 2:4, Eph.6:21-22, Col.4:7-8, Col.4:9
Reports and evidence  Acts 14:27, Acts 21:19, Acts 15:4,
                                        Acts 15:22, Acts 16:4
Communicating arrangements  2 Cor.8:21, 1 Cor.16:3
Letters of Recommendation  2 Cor.3:1, Rom.16:1-2, Acts 18:27
Travel help  Rom.15:24, Tit.3:12, Tit.3:13, 1 Cor.16:11
Our experience


## CHAPTER ELEVEN - ENCOURAGEMENT AND SUPPORT
Apostles bring helpful words which wake people up to God's
purposes and plans. As a result, barren or stalled situations
become fruitful as people reconnect with whom they are
meant to be.


Gophers.
God's words of life change things
Encouraged by sharing experiences
Releasing people – giving permission
Encouragement and practical help
Waking up – starting again
Remind and recall  2 Pet.3:1-2, Jn.15:15, Jn.14:26, 1 Jn.2:20, 27
Releasing a new atmosphere
Resetting culture
Investing in people  Prov.30:28, Isa.54:2
Enlarged hearts  Jn.3:8
Labourers in the market place  Matt.20:1-16, 2 Cor.6:13
Bringing overview and strategy
Identifying and resourcing
A changing environment
Re-imagining church

Paul's example of encouragement  2 Cor.10:8, 1 Cor.9:2,
            2  Cor.1:6,  Rom.1:11,  1  Thess.3:2,  Eph.3:2,
            Eph.4:29, 2 Cor.11:28
Mutual support  Rom.16:1, 2 Cor.11:9, Phil.4:16, Phil.2:25,
                                            2 Cor.8:23
Mutual encouragement  2 Cor.7:6, Phil.2:19, 2 Tim.1:4,
                        Rom.1:12, Rom.15:32, Eph.4:16

## CHAPTER TWELVE - DISTURBING AND DISRUPTING
One role of apostles is to disturb. They disturb old paradigms.
They go in and break things up that have lost their relevancy.
When things have lost their point, something needs to be
done. Apostles make adjustments - they characteristically
come in and break down any walls of religion, that have built
up in the life of the church.

Moles
Routines and bad habits
Breaking down bad thinking  2 Cor.10:8, 13:10
Wrong competitive thinking  1 Cor.1:12
Wrong complimentary thinking
Collaborative thinking  Ps.133:1

## CHAPTER THIRTEEN - HIDDEN TREASURE
God uses apostles to bring people out of darkness, like hidden
treasure and wonderful jewels, to use for His glory. Isa.45:3

A Treasure found in God  Job 28:1-11
Dug up by Jesus  Mt.13:44, Lk.19:10
A mining operation  John 15:5, Acts 1:8, Isa.45:1, Ezr.1:1-4,
                                            Heb.3:1
Twelve precious jewels  Rev.21:11
Treasures of Britain
Moles find treasure
Under our very noses

## CHAPTER FOURTEEN - TEAM

We all are in a team of God's choosing. There are people who God has called to be team to us, just as there are others, to whom He calls us to be team. God doesn't want apostles to work alone but with others in the territories assigned to them. We should expect to see teams emerging around us.

Our experience
Team is needed  Prov.27:17
Getting teams started
Male and female perspectives  Gal.3:26-28, 2 Cor.11:2
A company of women  Ps.68:11, Ps.68:19-20, Isa 40:9
An army of grandmothers  Mal.4:6
The mighty men who help us
A team comes together
Raw materials  1 Sam.22:2
A quality team  1 Ch.12:38, 1 Ch.12:39-40
Mutual help  Lk.6:38
Visionary names  1 Ch.11:35, 1 Ch.11:26-30, Acts 4:36
Woven Together  Col.2:2
Partnerships
New things

## PART FOUR - PRESENTING

How apostles help us to get ready for the final outcome, when we are presented as a beautiful, holy Bride of Christ, in a deep communion of relationships with God and one another.

## CHAPTER FIFTEEN - PRESENTING THE BRIDE

The church can be understood as the bride of Christ getting herself ready for her wedding day. Apostles help her in her preparations.

The New Jerusalem  Rev.19:7, Rev.19:9, Rev.21:2, Rev.21:14,
1 Cor.12:27

Making herself ready  1 Jn.3:2, 1 Jn.3:3, Phil.3:21, Rev.19:8
The father of the bride  Eph.5:30, Eph 5:31
A mystery  Eph.5:32, Eph.3:3-5, Rev.21:2
The work of the Trinity  Eph.3:20-21, Eph.5:27, SS.2:10,
            Eph.5:25, Gal.5:22-23, Eph.1:13-14,
            Rom.8:23 -26, Rev.22:17, Gal.4:6
The Ascension gifts  2 Cor.1:24, Eph.5:27
Paul the match-maker  2 Cor.11:2, Col.1:28, 2 Cor.12:19,
                                      2 Cor.13:9
Esther's beauty preparations  Es.1:8-12
The royal bride  Ps.45:10-17, Ps.45:13-14, Heb.1:8-9, Ps.45:10,
                                      Ps.45:11
Treasure in jars of clay  1 Cor.1:26-27, 1 Cor.6:10-11, 2 Cor.5:7,
                                      2 Cor.4:7
Tamar – restoring order  Gen. 38, Luke 18:1-8, 1 Cor.12:28

# LIST OF IMAGES

**Perfume bottle**
https://pxhere.com/en/photo/1212813
**Tree Stump and Green shoot**
Image by Mabel Amber, who will one day from Pixabay
**Scent Flowers in vase**
Photo by form PxHere
**Umbrellas**
Image by Hana Harencarova from Pixabay
**Herd of Bulls**
Wood bison or mountain...bison athabascae.jpg
Courtesy of:          commons.wikimedia.org
**Yoked oxen pulling cart**
Photo by form PxHere
**Towel and Bowl**
Photo by form PxHere
**Harvest**
Sagarjitkar, CC BY-SA 4.0
<https://creativecommons.org/licenses/by-sa/4.0>, via
Wikimedia Commons
**Two Donkeys**
donkeys-animal-the-countryside-742115.jpg
Courtesy of:                pixabay.com
**Open Door**
Image by Manfred Antranias Zimmer from Pixabay
**Cyrus Mission**
1989 Product Catalogue
**Keys**
Bunch of keys from https://www.hippopx.com/sl/query?q=keys
**Prayer Walking**
feet-lady-walking-sandles-female-538245.jpg
Courtesy of:                pixabay.com
**Tin cans**
Image by monicore from Pixabay
**Parenting Father with daughter**
Girl-father-portrait-e...-outdoor-1641215.jpg

**Training Cucumbers**
The Neal's Homestead
**Parenting Discovery Bubbles**
Photo by form PxHere
**Underground animals Mole popping up**
Mole-nature-animals-molehills-13299.jpg
**Rabbits**
Image by Joanjo Puertos Munoz from Pixabay
**Writing a letter**
Image by Free photos from Pixabay
**Gophers**
Image by Наталья Коллегова from Pixabay
**Toolbox Neat tools**
Photo: Wooden board with hanged hand tools by Marco
Verch under Creative Commons 2.0
**Rooftops Whitby**
image by <a
href="http://www.freeimageslive.co.uk/free_stock_image/english
-houses-jpg" target="_blank"> freeimageslive.co.uk -
photoeverywhere</a>
**Mole hills**
Image by **Ulrike Mai** from **Pixabay**
**Precious Jewels**
https://www.publicdomainpictures.net/pictures/160000/velka/ce
ltic-jewels.jpg
**Painting Set**
https://www.flickr.com/photos/didmyself/9390588145
Daniel Kulinski  Flickr
**Line of fishermen**
https://www.flickr.com/photos/volvob12b/33426274976
**Woven Basket**
terryatkinson.typepad.com
**Placed in the Train of His Glory**
https://www.pinterest.co.uk/pin/397724210828646039/
**Presenting the Bride**
Courtesy of Matt Dartford Photography
**Bookmarks, Treasures of Britain, Bain family outing and
The Missing Piece** by Mary Bain

# BOOKS FROM
# OPEN WELLS PUBLISHING

## BY THE SAME AUTHORS

Becoming Multi-flavoured Church
Singing over Havering
Prayer Walking around Redbridge
Launching after Lockdown
Sentness

Poems by Mary Bain:
My Song Matters
Beyond the Door

*Available from **www.lulu.com** or **Amazon***

God on the Move
A fifty minute film –
Youtube search for
"God on the Move - Havering"
*Welcome Network youtube channel*

*Other resources available on welcomenetwork.org*

To God be the Glory!

Printed in Great Britain
by Amazon